73025 COH AMOS LG   30127304 TPR ANSON LG   W10468... ...2309
R ATTAKORAH LG   30111290 TPR ATTWOOD LG   30062... ...1628
KER LG   30138285 TPR BARKER LG   30152224 TPR BARRE... ...ETT
T LG   30146504 TPR BEELUR LG   25193437 LCOH BELAS... ...ICK
EAL LG   30061719 LCPL BLAKE LG   30150083 TPR BLAND LG   25193299 LCOH BLISS LG
OH BOSWELL LG   30070904 TPR BOWMAN LG   25095653 LCOH BRADBURY LG   30130576
WO1 BROWN LG   25139815 LCOH BROWN LG   25181314 LCPL BROWN LG   25105820 LCPL
G   561797 CAPT CARTER LG   25008814 CPL CARTER LG   30077345 TPR CARTWRIGHT LG
SSGT CLARK RLC   30069091 MUSN CLARKE LG   25088615 LCOH CLAYDEN LG   30062013
OLLIS-SMITH LG   30115993 TPR COMLEY LG   30157562 TPR CONNOLL LG   30058609 TPR
24896135 COH DANIELS LG   30074251 TPR DARCY LG   24869527 CPL DARCY LG   30075576
G   25133088 MUSN DIGGLE LG   25161147 MUSN DOLOR LG   25188145 LCPL DOMINEY LG
D LG   25135042 LCPL DUGGAN LG   30094623 TPR DUMBRELL LG   30096340 TPR DURNO
7796 TPR ELLISTON-JONES LG   25193808 LCPL EMSLEY LG   30098084 TPR ERHAHIEMEN
3653 TPR FLYNN LG   30063158 TPR FORSYTH LG   30140514 TPR FOX LG   W0833883 WO1
WAY LG   25182609 LCPL GALUVAKADUA LG   30140481 TPR GARDNER LG   30060634 TPR
LG   30127199 TPR GILLHAM LG   30027293 LCPL GLASS LG   25227743 LCPL GOODACRE LG
119104 LCPL GRAY LG   30141755 TPR GREEN LG   30070544 TPR GRIFFIN LG   30115108 TPR
LG   30098490 TPR HAIGH LG   25217461 LCPL HAIGH AGC(SPS)   30038275 TPR HALE LG
TPR HARTREE LG   30106392 TPR HARVEY LG   30056373 TPR HASTINGS LG   30084075 TPR
NDERSON LG   25101944 LCPL HEYWOOD LG   30014993 PTE HIGGINS AGC(SPS)   25115001
IFFE LG   25182640 LCPL HIRST LG   30036973 TPR HOCKEY LG   25118258 LCPL HOLLAND
N LG   30070502 LT HORNE LG   30083315 TPR HOWARD LG   25037915 LCOH HOWELL LG
REYS LG   25153226 LCPL JAMES LG   25167981 LCPL JANI LG   25065953 COH JAWORSKI LG
PR KENNARDSMITH LG   25133649 MUSN KENNEDY LG   W1045756 MUSN KENNEDY LG
567 LCOH LACEY LG   W1056283 MUSN LAMB LG   25219103 TPR LAWRENCE LG   25099816
ONG LG   25098991 LCOH LOREY LG   30145329 TPR LUGG LG   25221041 LCPL MALANEY
58020 TPR MARCHANT LG   30114220 MUSN MARSHALL LG   30095508 MUSN MARSHALL
LG   30088836 TPR MATHEWS LG   30088836 TPR MATHEWS - PALAPOIKAYIL LG   25159675
CVICAR LG   563989 MAJ MEREDITH HARDY LG   25191867 TPR METCALFE LG   30126920
NEWELL LG   30109211 TPR NEWTON LG   30156338 TPR NIBA AMBE LG   25156745 LCOH
G   30150010 TPR OSBORN LG   30051334 TPR O'SHEA LG   30054518 TPR OWUSU-MENSAH
25092408 MUSN PATTERSON LG   24773156 CAPT PAYNE LG   25199151 TPR PEARCE LG
COH POWELL LG   24930006 SCPL PRESTON LG   30030559 TPR PRITCHARD LG   25129880
OH RAIWALE LG   25182607 LCPL RAJ LG   30040117 TPR RASTRICK LG   25113224 LCOH
N LG   30132310 TPR ROBINSON LG   25101934 CPL ROCKEY LG   24748221 CAPT ROGERS LG
TPR ROOPCHAND LG   30141087 TPR ROUTER LG   24885225 LCPL ROYSTON LG   30126923
DERS LG   25152991 MUSN SANDFORD LG   30128627 LCOH SAURARA LG   25132685 TPR
30140196 TPR SHORT LG   25127860 LCPL SILLS LG   25183224 LCPL SINCLAIR LG   30012594
ITH LG   24884074 SGT SPARKS LG   25231319 TPR SPENCER LG   L8515588 COH STAFFORD
CAPT STEWART LG   30088453 TPR STOKES LG   30081108 TPR STOKES LG   25075243 COH
G   30011369 TPR THACKER LG   30096160 TPR THOMPSON LG   25224531 LCPL TINGLE LG
G   25232930 TPR VAN DER WALT LG   30098614 TPR VEEN LG   30059513 TPR VENESS LG
AJ WALL LG   554812 CAPT WALLIS LG   24793215 SGT WALSH LG   30058578 TPR WALTON
30132194 TPR WEBB LG   30106071 TPR WEBB LG   25148845 LCPL WELSH LG   25030501
R WHITE LG   25064724 COH WILLIAMS LG   30129670 TPR WILLIAMS LG   24433493 LCPL
OS LG   24877652 COH WYARD LG   30081841 TPR YARROW LG   24905384 COH YOUNG LG

UNIQUELY BRITISH

A year in the life of the Household Cavalry
from the Royal Wedding to the Diamond Jubilee

This book is dedicated to all those Household Cavalrymen who have lost their lives or been injured whilst serving their country.

UNIQUELY BRITISH

A year in the life of the Household Cavalry
from the Royal Wedding to the Diamond Jubilee

Foreword by
Her Majesty The Queen

Edited by Lieutenant Colonel Dan Hughes

Written by The Officers of the Household Cavalry & Christopher Joll

TRICORN
BOOKS

UNIQUELY BRITISH
A year in the life of the Household Cavalry
from the Royal Wedding to the Diamond Jubilee

Design © 131 Design Ltd
www.131design.org
Published by Tricorn Books
www.tricornbooks.co.uk

A CIP catalogue record for this book is available from
The British Library.

Edited by Lieutenant Colonel Dan Hughes.
Sub-editor: Captain Thomas Davie.
Written by The Officers of the Household Cavalry & Christopher Joll.
Design & layout: Dan Bernard & Gail Baird, Tricorn Books.
Photographs © Julian Calder, Dan Bernard,
Jasper Dalgliesh, Chris Allerton, Anya Campbell, Sergeant Jason Nilsson,
Mitzi de Margary, Gail Baird, Captain Simon Lukas, Lance Corporal of Horse Dan Short,
Tom Craig, Bob Martin, Tom Lovelock, Nico Morgan, Heathcliff O'Malley.
With images by kind permission of MOD-Crown©
©www.royalimages.com Julian Calder
Project Officers: Captain Martin Dansey and Captain Simon Lukas.
Text © HCMR

ISBN 978-0-9571074-0-3
Published 2012 by Tricorn Books,
a trading name of 131 Design Ltd.
131 High Street, Old Portsmouth, PO1 2HW

Printed & bound by W&G Baird Ltd in the UK

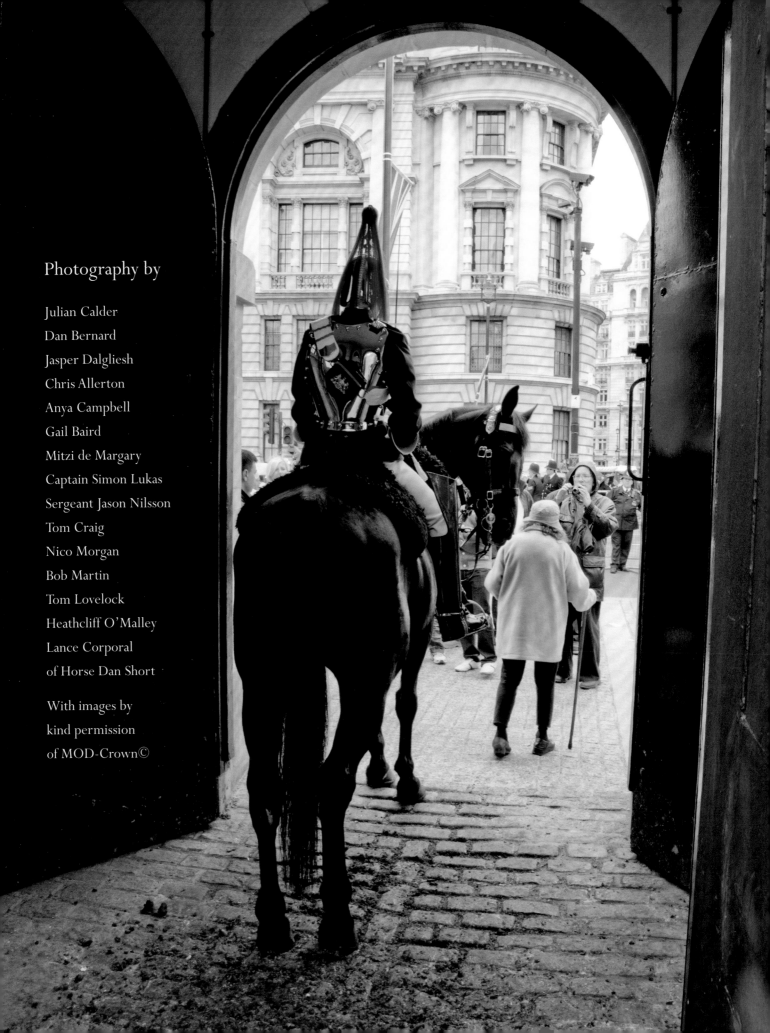

Photography by

Julian Calder
Dan Bernard
Jasper Dalgliesh
Chris Allerton
Anya Campbell
Gail Baird
Mitzi de Margary
Captain Simon Lukas
Sergeant Jason Nilsson
Tom Craig
Nico Morgan
Bob Martin
Tom Lovelock
Heathcliff O'Malley
Lance Corporal
of Horse Dan Short

With images by
kind permission
of MOD-Crown©

Every Household Cavalryman is first and foremost an operational soldier: proudly wearing the operational service medals from Former Yugoslavia, Northern Ireland, Afghanistan and Iraq.

Contents

As Colonel-in-Chief of the two distinguished Regiments that make up the Household Cavalry, The Life Guards and The Blues and Royals, I have been able to observe over many years the Household Cavalry Mounted Regiment carrying out State Ceremonial and Public Duties to the highest of standards, a role that reflects upon the distinctive characteristics and heritage of the United Kingdom. This volume celebrates that tradition of excellence, built up during 350 years of loyal service to the Crown, and which forms a unique part of this Country's military tradition. This heritage reflects the values, standards and actions of the Regiments on active service and is continued today by the Household Cavalry Regiment on current operations, for which they prepare to deploy to Afghanistan in 2013.

The individual and collective skills of man and horse, which the book portrays, will be seen extensively during this, my Diamond Jubilee year, but we should also remember that vital operational role of the Household Cavalry during times of conflict. I am therefore pleased to acknowledge this tribute to its former and current soldiers, and especially to those who have died or been wounded in the service of our Nation. That is why the cause which the book supports is a noble one, and has my full support.

Elizabeth R

June, 2012.

INTRODUCTION

HRH The Princess Royal KG KT GCVO
Colonel The Blues and Royals

General the Lord Guthrie of Craigiebank GCB LVO OBE DL
Colonel The Life Guards

The public's perception of the role of the Household Cavalry is largely driven by the frequent sight on London's streets of soldiers on black horses in full ceremonial dress with helmets, swords and cuirasses glinting in the sun. Whilst it is true that, traditionally, the first duty of the Regiments of the Household Cavalry was to provide close protection to our Sovereign and Colonel-in-Chief, expressed today through the delivery of matchless mounted and dismounted ceremonial duties, it should not be forgotten that the Household Cavalry has always been required to perform on the front line in the defence of our country. Consequently we have been engaged in every major war, and most of the minor ones, over the 350 years since our formation around the time of the Restoration of the Monarchy in 1660.

Warfare is rarely glamorous, so it is difficult to illustrate in a book of this type the commitment and sacrifice that has been and continues to be made by the officers and soldiers of the Household Cavalry in the defence of this country. We hope that in the pages that follow, and in particular through the interviews with our soldiers, you the reader will fully appreciate the dual role of the Household Cavalry in both the ceremonial and operational arenas. The imbalance in the photography between these two roles should not be allowed to hide the fact that every Household Cavalryman is a fighting soldier first – and the troops participating in ceremonial parades are fully trained, operational troops who may only recently have been in armoured vehicles in the harsh terrain of Afghanistan.

The proceeds from the sale of this book will be used to fund the launch of the Household Cavalry Foundation, a new charity that will bring together all our welfare activities, whether in support of serving soldiers, operational casualties, veterans or even our horses. We thank you for your support of this cause and hope you enjoy this new book about our unique organisation.

Colonel
The Life Guards

Colonel
The Blues and Royals

"Supporting our soldiers, casualties, veterans, horses and heritage"

*T*he Household Cavalry Foundation has been set up to care for the soldiers, families, horses and heritage of Britain's Senior Regiment. It will allow a much needed evolution in the way we support serving and retired members of the Household Cavalry and their dependants. Whether caring for soldiers injured on operations, or providing relief to veterans and their families, the Household Cavalry Foundation will provide an umbrella of support to the Regimental family. The Foundation has five charitable aims:

- **Soldier Welfare:** Provide support to, and promote the efficiency of, serving members of the Household Cavalry. Whether to relieve hardship or distress, assist those injured on training or in peacetime, or to encourage sport, adventure training or charitable endeavour, the Foundation will care for all 900 soldiers of the Household Cavalry serving at home or abroad.

- **Casualty Welfare:** Provide financial support to injured soldiers and their families, including those who have lost their lives on active service.

- **Veterans Welfare:** Relieve past members of the Household Cavalry and their dependants who are in need, hardship or distress, or those who have become seriously ill, or have broader welfare needs.

- **Horse Welfare:** Provide financial and other support to organisations and individuals involved in the welfare of our horses.

- **Heritage and Tradition:** Maintain the fabric of the Household Cavalry by preserving our heritage and ethos, museums and archives, and regimental property.

www.hcavfoundation.org

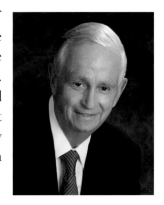

The Household Cavalry has captured the imagination of the public for longer than any of us can remember. Those of us who see them in action are acutely aware that they are watching something which is both remarkable and unique. I have long been an admirer of all that the Household Cavalry and the Household Division stands for, whether it is the highest standards of excellence and steadiness they display on parade, or the courage and professionalism with which they fight in today's complex operations.

I hope that you will enjoy this rare look behind the scenes of the Household Cavalry. It is a timely and ground-breaking book, and one that not only celebrates a unique period in British ceremonial history, but also provides a unique view of the pageantry and heritage for which Great Britain is so famous.

The Household Cavalry Foundation is a new flagship charity to provide care and support to all parts of the Household Cavalry family, whether it is serving soldiers, veterans, casualties or retired horses. It is therefore fitting that a proud global brand, JW Marriott, should be supporting the Household Cavalry Foundation in achieving its charitable aims.

I hope you enjoy this exclusive account of life in the Household Cavalry, and that it helps convey to you the matchless military and ceremonial inheritance that is Uniquely British.

J.W. Marriott Jr

J.W. Marriott Jnr.

UNIQUELY BRITISH

A year in the life of the Household Cavalry
from the Royal Wedding to the Diamond Jubilee

CHAPTER 1

The Royal Wedding

Friday 29th April 2011 could have been just another Friday in London; tourists jostling for position outside Buckingham Palace, busy Londoners making their way to work, and the soldiers and horses of the Household Cavalry preparing for another day.

But this Friday was different. His Royal Highness Prince William of Wales, one of our fellow officers and second-in-line to the throne, would be marrying Miss Catherine Middleton in Westminster Abbey. Over one million people were expected to be lining the processional route, with the ceremony and festivities being covered by 8,500 journalists and broadcast to one of the largest-ever global TV audiences.

Playing a leading role in this historic event were over 200 horses and soldiers of the Household Cavalry Mounted Regiment. Our main role was to escort the bride and groom, Her Majesty The Queen and other members of the Royal Family from Westminster Abbey to Buckingham Palace after the ceremony.

Although the wedding was not a full state occasion, it featured many traditional ceremonial aspects, including the use of the state carriages of the Royal Mews, the Household Cavalry and Foot Guards. As Prince William was not the heir apparent to the throne, many details were left to the couple to decide, including a specific request for four friends within the Regiment to command their personal escort during the procession.

Despite the high profile nature of the event, this was not the first Royal Wedding we have been involved in during our long history: the marriage of King Charles II to Catherine of Braganza in 1662 takes that award. As Samuel Pepys reported in his diary:

The Troops of Horse were drawn up in Hyde Park, a very noble sight in all capacities. Most of that great body had formerly been at war, and so were more than fit to be guard and escort to the couple most excellent.

The same was true in 2011. On the day of the Royal Wedding, over 120 members of the Household Cavalry were deployed on the frontline in Helmand Province in Afghanistan. The fact that it was D Squadron, Prince William's former squadron, made it all the more poignant.

Although it was not our first Royal Wedding, it was one of the biggest. None of us had actually taken part in a parade of this size before, although some of the old boys remembered the wedding of the Prince and Princess of Wales 30 years previously. All we knew was that it was big – and when we left the barracks we realised just how big as we heard a thundering swell of noise coming from the centre of Hyde Park, where huge crowds had gathered to watch live footage of the wedding ceremony which was already under way in the Abbey. We hadn't gone more than 200 metres before the crowds were 10 deep on each side of the road and still a kilometre from the main parade route.

However, whilst the public expects to see the style, elegance and precision that are the hallmarks of British pageantry, we had made no such assumptions. From the Commanding Officer to the most junior trooper, there was a sense of trepidation as we departed the barracks to take up our positions outside the Abbey.

Not all had gone according to plan during rehearsals. The horses had refused to settle, especially when confronted with flag-waving soldiers in Hyde Park. With huge crowds expected on the big day we became more and more concerned!

In the end, the painstaking time we spent in preparation – from cleaning and checking the kit to early morning rehearsals – meant that for

Above: 'Everybody scatter!' The horses take matters into their own hands. Part of the challenge of the Royal Wedding was the effect on the horses of the huge crowds and noise. As we undergo crowd training in Hyde Park, members of the band try replicating the noise of one million spectators! There were mixed reactions but the horses became more tolerant after much practising. *Previous page*: The newly-wed Duke and Duchess of Cambridge are escorted home by the Officer Commanding the Captain's Escort.

the most part everything went smoothly on the day. Our abiding memories are the wall of noise from the cheering crowds and military bands on the Mall as we approached Buckingham Palace, and the enormous sense of relief as we entered Hyde Park Barracks after a successful parade: definitely one to tell the grandchildren about.

At Horse Guards, the Duke of Cambridge salutes, and the Duchess bows her head, to acknowledge both the Guidon of The Blues and Royals and the salute of the Queen's Life Guard. The Guidon was used in place of The Blues and Royals Sovereign's Standard as the latter was accompanying Her Majesty on the return journey to Buckingham Palace. Horse Guards is the historical entrance to the Royal residences in central London, and the Sovereign's Life Guard has guarded these gates every day for over 350 years.

One Troop of The Blues and Royals
Squadron prepares for the parade
ahead. Note the tail bandages to
ensure immaculate presentation
even in the early mornings when
spectators will be few.

'The horses begin to settle.' Members of the Regiment attempt to mimic the expected crowds at the Royal Wedding to prepare the horses for the 'wall of noise'.

'All the Queen's horses.' A carriage and horses from the Royal Mews join the Household Cavalry for combined training on Rotten Row. The Escorting Officers can be seen around the carriage.

'Charge!' The Sovereign's Escort conducts a full dress rehearsal in Hyde Park before the Royal Wedding.

An early start to achieve perfection. The Regiment forms up for an Early Morning Rehearsal for the Royal Wedding. Even at this hour, each soldier and horse is thoroughly inspected for safety and cleanliness.

The rehearsing Captain's Escort waits patiently. On the day of the Royal Wedding, they will escort the newly married couple back to Buckingham Palace. A Captain's Escort, smaller than that for the Sovereign, is used for other members of the Royal Family.

Soldiers of The Life Guards (left) and Officers of The Blues and Royals (right) use a 'buddy buddy' system to dress. The Officers are fitting their gold crossbelts which are only worn in the presence of senior Royalty.

The cold break of day. We do an Early Morning Rehearsal so as not to impact on busy city commuters.

'Homeward bound.' The Blues and Royals return to Hyde Park Barracks after the Early Morning Rehearsal for the Royal Wedding.

'Running like clockwork.' LCpl Raj checks his watch while Tpr Jones and LCpl Headley contemplate the parade ahead.

Top: 'Who's leading who?' A horse of The Life Guards with its sheepskin-covered saddle is led up to the parade square from the Squadron stables. ***Above***: Inspection over and helmets off for one last scratch of the head before the Regiment leaves barracks for the Royal Wedding.

Meanwhile, on the Front Line

Whilst we in the Mounted Regiment braved the crowds on the streets of London, our friends in the Household Cavalry Regiment (HCR) were dealing with very different, and potentially more lethal situations, in Helmand Province, Afghanistan.

By coincidence, the Squadron that was deployed in Afghanistan on the day of the Royal Wedding ('D' Squadron

HCR) was the one Prince William had served with during his time as a reconnaissance troop leader in the Household Cavalry in 2007. These photographs are of his old Squadron on combat missions in Helmand on the day of his wedding. In one form or another, officers and soldiers of the Household Cavalry have been on the front line in Afghanistan from the beginning of the conflict and, to date, the Regiment has deployed on five operational tours, with the likelihood of a further tour in 2013. Along with virtually every other unit which has deployed to Afghanistan, the Regiment has taken many casualties, both killed and wounded-in-action. During the campaign, the work of our officers and soldiers has been recognised by the award of two Conspicuous Gallantry Crosses and three Military Crosses.

It is perhaps worth reflecting that all Household Cavalry soldiers are first and foremost fighting soldiers and, almost uniquely in the British Army, train for operational and mounted ceremonial roles. It is this flexibility which has allowed us to remain at the forefront of modern combat operations and maintain the high standards of excellence and professionalism for which we are renowned.

Above left: Troops watch the Royal Wedding at Camp Bastion. ***Left***: A Conspicuous Galantry Cross on parade. ***Opposite***: 'On patrol.' 'D' Squadron the Household Cavalry Regiment in the 'Green Zone' on the day of the Royal Wedding near Gereshk, Helmand Province, Afghanistan.

LCpl Selby practising his Pashto with a local on patrol near Gereshk, Helmand Province, Afghanistan.

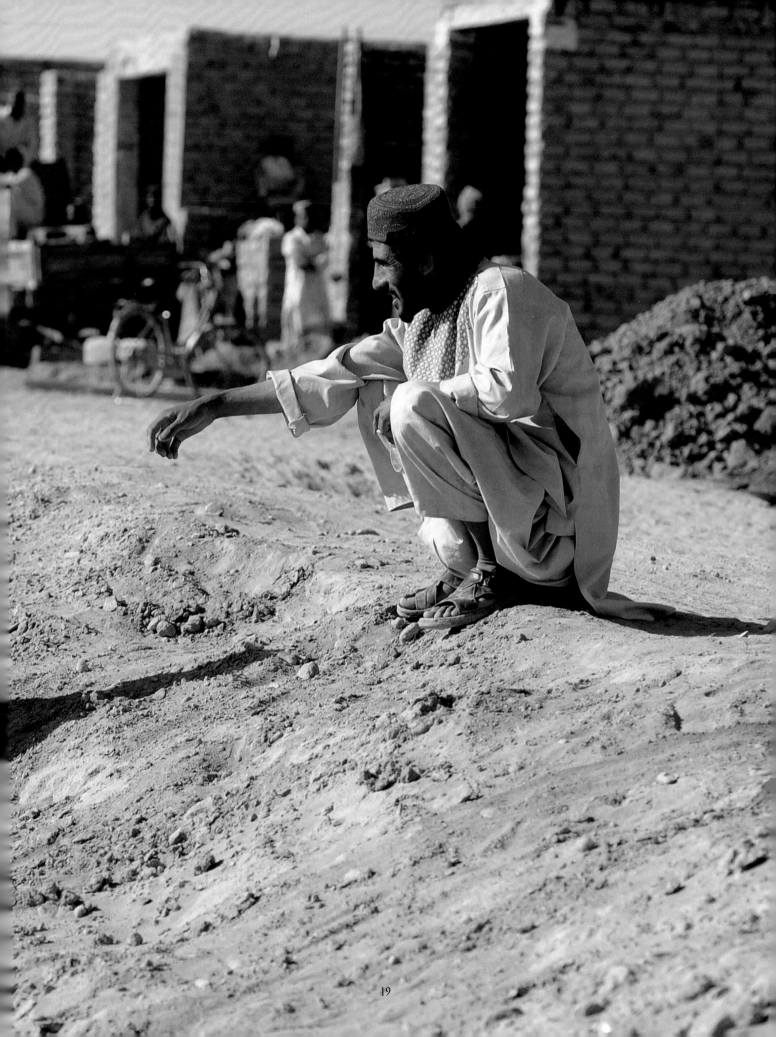

'Duties to be done.' Here the Standard Party, followed by the Silver Stick, departs Hyde Park Barracks en route to Westminster Abbey as the crowds begin to swell.

'Calm before the storm.' A member of the Queen's Life Guard surveys the immaculate lines of Guardsmen on the morning of the Royal Wedding.

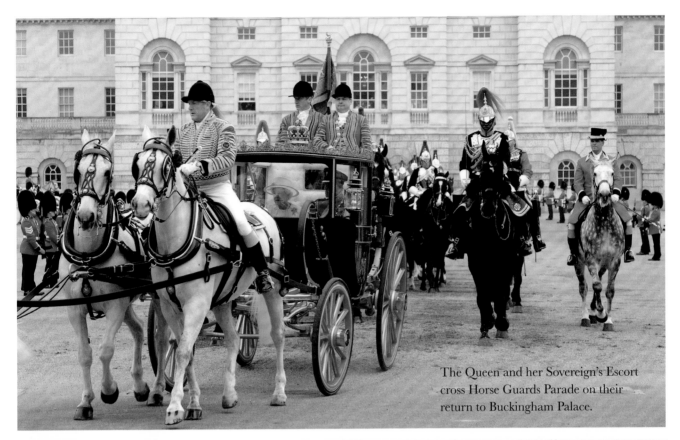

The Queen and her Sovereign's Escort cross Horse Guards Parade on their return to Buckingham Palace.

'Home for tea and medals.' The Household Cavalry Mounted Regiment return to barracks through the euphoric crowds.

Wearing the uniform of a Blues and Royals Officer, Prince Henry of Wales, or Captain Harry Wales as the Regiment knows him, accompanies the bridesmaids and pageboys back to Buckingham Palace.

The happy couple – The Duke and Duchess of Cambridge.

'A job well done.' Members of The Life Guards Squadron after turning their horses in.

CHAPTER 2

Learning the Ropes

Whilst taking part in the Royal Wedding was a unique and thrilling experience, it is not a routine occurrence for the Household Cavalry Mounted Regiment. The provision of fully trained soldiers and horses for mounted State Ceremonial and Public Duties is our core function, and the story that lies behind the delivery of that duty is something that the public almost never sees or hears about.

The story of how woolly, untrained horses grazing in a field, and raw recruits fresh from school or university, end up on parade in central London, glinting from helmet to hoof, is one full of long hours, aches and pains, the odd tumble and a considerable amount of hard graft.

For our horses, the story starts in Ireland, where the majority enjoy their early lives. 'Cavalry Blacks' are, in the main, traditional crossbreeds of Irish Draught and Thoroughbred and normally stand at 16.2 hands or over. A buying commission is convened twice a year to search for horses of the right type and colour that will look and perform well on ceremonial parades. They are purchased in Ireland at 3-5 years of age and are predominantly black with some white markings. Exceptions are the 'greys' for trumpeters, the all-black Officers' chargers, and the Drum Horses – Shires and Clydesdales – which are specially selected and trained to carry the heavy solid silver kettledrums.

For those horses selected, their training is done at the Defence Animal Centre at Melton Mowbray in Leicestershire, or in-house and at the Household Cavalry Training Wing in Windsor. The first letter of their name denotes their age, just like a vehicle registration number. In 2012, the Diamond Jubilee year, the letter is 'M', so names such as Majesty and Monarch have already been chosen, with other names selected from our Regimental history or battle honours, or even suggested by the public!

A Regimental and Squadron number is also stamped onto the hooves of each horse, a tradition dating back to when horses killed on the battlefield had their hooves removed by the Farriers to allow replacement horses to be purchased.

For the soldiers the story is very different. Their military career starts with 14 weeks of Phase 1 (Basic Training) and Phase 2 (Special-to-Arm Training), the latter taking place with the remainder of the Royal Armoured Corps at Bovington in Dorset. Upon posting to the Mounted Regiment, soldiers must then train for the role of Mounted Dutyman involving a 10-week 'Khaki' and 5-week 'Kit' Ride where they learn the fundamentals of equitation and horse welfare. Riding and stable management are covered in depth, as well as the inevitable kit cleaning that forms such a large part of life when on ceremonial duty. As many as 95% of the soldiers will have had no prior experience of horses when they arrive and the training is physically and mentally arduous. The Ride culminates with a Passing Out Parade at Hyde Park Barracks in front of an invited VIP and is attended by the families and friends of the trainees who have achieved the requisite standard. It is a proud moment for them, buoyed with an enormous sense of achievement and relief.

The Mounted Regiment itself also has to go through a 'pass out'. This is the Annual Inspection by the Major General Commanding the Household Division and is normally the first main parade of the year before the ceremonial season gets into full stride. The parade, the purpose of which is to ensure the Household Cavalry Mounted Regiment is 'fit for task', comprises virtually the entire Regiment forming-up and demonstrating a range of mounted drills in Hyde Park.

Previous page: LCpl Smith, with the green helmet silk of a trainee, waits his turn. Having passed the course he will wear the coloured silk of his Regiment. *Opposite*: 'Turning and changing across the school by sections.' Working in a section of four teaches those in training basic control of their horse, paramount when on parade.

Above: Trainees muck out at the Household Cavalry Training Wing in Windsor, the first task of every new day. *Left*: Caring for your horse is one of the first lessons taught at the Training Wing, and will remain with the men throughout their time at the Mounted Regiment.

Opposite top: Attention to detail and pride in appearance are instilled in the men from day one. Chalk is used to whiten any patches on the predominantly black horses. *Middle*: 'Ride, stand to your horses.' Khaki Ride trainees present their mounts for inspection prior to another morning's lesson. *Bottom*: The Commanding Officer hands Service Dress hats to newly qualified soldiers. This symbolic moment means that the men have reached the standard required and will progress to Kit Ride. The sheer delight is evident.

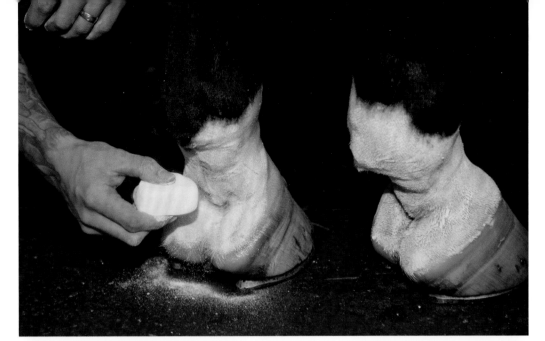

33

Horses exercise
in Hyde Park.

Kit Ride. This is a gruelling five week course of early mornings in the saddle and late nights spent polishing kit. After this the officers and soldiers will have ridden in every type of uniform, including the famous jackboots and state helmet. They will also have an understanding of the basic day-to-day parades that the Regiment undertakes.

'It never rains, but it pours.' The Commanding Officer, Squadron Leaders, Riding Master, the Officer Commanding Training Wing and the Regimental Corporal Major cast a critical eye over members of Training Wing. If the trainees have not mastered the basics of equitation, then they will not fool this experienced crowd.

Cambian Patrol training.
The Cambian Patrol
is an Army-wide skills
competition held annually
in the Brecon Beacons.
The skills required are very
different from those of a
Mounted Dutyman, but
Household Cavalry soldiers
are dual-trained and can
employ whichever set
is required.

Trooper Collins leads his
Ride at the Training Wing.
Collins had a head start
in his training as he had
ridden before. The vast
majority of soldiers have
never even sat on a horse
before Khaki Ride.

This page top: Major General His Grace The Duke of Westminster inspects the Kit Ride Pass Off. This is a hugely proud moment for friends and family who have watched the transformation from recruit into Mounted Dutyman. ***Above***: 'Eyes Right.' The soldiers of Kit Ride practise their routine, followed by their instructors. ***Opposite page***: LCoH Glasgow eyeing up the next fence during a jumping lesson. Part of Khaki Ride is learning to jump, a terrifying prospect for the novice rider, although the soldiers always find the courage from somewhere!

The Commanding Officer at the head of the Regiment on the Major General's Inspection. This is the first parade of the Ceremonial Season and demonstrates that the Regiment is ready for all events to come. It is the culmination of weeks of horse inspections, kit inspections and drills which ensure we are up to standard after the long winter.

Top: The Quartermaster; Captain Nick Stewart; Regimental Administration Officer, Captain Martin Dansey; Regimental Veterinary Officer, Major Ann O'Flynn and Regimental Surgeon, Lieutenant Colonel Jedge Lewin riding on the Major General's Inspection. ***Above***: The Band of The Life Guards entertain the joggers in Hyde Park as they lead the Regiment home after the Major General's Inspection.

Major General George Norton, Commanding the Household Division, inspects The Blues and Royals on the Major General's Inspection.

A wide range of millinery on show as the Regimental Staff Officers bring up the rear on the Major General's Inspection.

CHAPTER 3

History & Heritage

The Household Cavalry consists of The Life Guards and The Blues and Royals (Royal Horse Guards and 1st Dragoons). These are the most senior Regiments in the British Army and since 1821, the Colonels-in-Chief have by tradition been the reigning monarch, currently Her Majesty The Queen.

Soldiers from the Regiments are split between two different units with two quite different roles. The Household Cavalry Regiment at Windsor has an operational role in mounted and dismounted reconnaissance and has seen service during most of Britain's conflicts, including the Falklands (1982), the Gulf (1990) and more recently operations in Bosnia, Kosovo, Iraq and Afghanistan.

Equipped with horses, the Household Cavalry Mounted Regiment in London has the unique privilege of carrying out mounted ceremonial and public duties on State and Royal occasions. All officers and soldiers are trained in both roles and rotate between the two Regiments throughout their careers.

The Household Cavalry has a long and rich history, maintaining a world-famous tradition dating back to 1660. At the time of the Restoration of the Monarchy, The Life Guards were formed from a group of royalists who had gone into exile with King Charles II after his defeat at the Battle of Worcester in

1652. Originally designated as five Troops of Horse Guards, they were reformed and re-designated the 1st and 2nd Life Guards in 1788, and amalgamated to form The Life Guards (1st and 2nd) in 1922 until 1928 when they were renamed The Life Guards. During a long history, The Life Guards have been deployed in a greater variety of combat roles than any other regiment of the British Army.

In contrast to the royalist roots of The Life Guards, The Blues and Royals trace their origins back to a unit of Oliver Cromwell's New Model Army, Unton Croke's Regiment of Horse. At the Restoration the regiment was renamed The Royal Horse Guards (The Blues), and although greatly favoured by King George III, who appointed himself a captain in the regiment, it was not until 1820 that King George IV designated them as Household Cavalry.

Thereafter they shared the duties of escorting the Sovereign with the two regiments of Life Guards. In 1969, The Royal Horse Guards (The Blues) was amalgamated with The Royal Dragoons (1st Dragoons), a regiment originally known as the Tangier Horse, which had been formed in 1661 by King Charles II to defend Tangier, a royal possession after the King's marriage to Catherine of Braganza. The battle honours of the Regiments that comprise today's Household Cavalry include every major and most of the minor conflicts of the past 350 years including the latest one, Iraq, which was awarded in 1991.

The Life Guards wear red tunics with white helmet plumes. The Blues and Royals wear blue tunics with red helmet plumes but this show of colour has not always been visible. During the Second World War the King's Life Guard was mounted in khaki uniforms. It was only for the wedding of the then Princess Elizabeth in 1947 that the splendour of full ceremonial uniform returned.

Each Regiment has a Sovereign's Standard and three Squadron (or Union) Standards; The Blues and Royals also have a Guidon. The Standards and Guidon carry

Previous page: An enduring symbol of power. The Regimental Corporal Major's whip carries the Garter Star, a reflection of the Regiment's loyalty to the Monarch.

Left to right, from top: The impressive chest of CoH Andrew Radford CGC displays his Operational Service Medals for Northern Ireland, Iraq and Afghanistan, where he won a Conspicuous Gallantry Cross.

The shabraque of an Officer of The Life Guards displaying the names of the Regiment's battle honours.

The unique black plume of a Farrier.

The red-plumed bicorn of the Regimental Veterinary Officer.

A shabraque of an Officer of The Blues and Royals.

The black-plumed bicorn of the Regimental Surgeon. Household Cavalry doctors have the unique honour of becoming an Officer of the Regiment.

The two Regimental Standards given by the Sovereign and displaying the battle honours.

The axe carried on parade by the Regimental Farriers.

49

the Regimental battle honours and are consecrated when presented to the Regiments every 10 years, last performed in May 2003 by Her Majesty The Queen. Battle honours are also carried on Officers' shabraques, a highly decorated embroidered saddlecloth worn when members of the Royal Family are present on parade.

The Farriers of both Regiments by tradition carry axes on parade. The purpose of the axes was to enable the Farriers to dispatch wounded horses on the battlefield and then – for accounting purposes – remove the hoof carrying the Regimental Number.

The Colonels of the Regiments are currently The Princess Royal, Colonel of The Blues and Royals, and General the Lord Guthrie of Craigiebank, Colonel of The Life Guards, and both are appointed by Her Majesty The Queen. They also hold the title of Gold Stick and are 'In Waiting' to Her Majesty in rotation each month. The appointment of Gold Stick, named after the staff of office, a gold-topped ebony cane, was originally created in 1678 by King Charles II for an officer to be in 'close attendance' to the King at all times and entrusted with his safety.

Another court appointment, that of Silver Stick in Waiting, is currently a serving full Colonel who deputises for the Gold Sticks on day-to-day business. This post was also created by King Charles II, and he carries a silver-topped ebony cane as his staff of office when on parade.

The rank and insignia of Non-Commissioned Officers (NCOs) in the Household Cavalry are unique. Since Life Guard soldiers were originally private gentlemen, the word Corporal is used instead of Sergeant (derived from the Latin for servant). Warrant Officer and Non-Commissioned ranks are therefore titled Staff Corporal, Squadron Corporal Major etc. Rank badges are also different and, in Full Dress, denoted by aiguillettes worn from the left shoulder, rather than by the chevrons and crowns used by the rest of the Army.

On State occasions and when members of the Royal Family are present, the two Household Cavalry Bands, the Kettledrummers and the Trumpeters wear identical velvet 'jockey caps' and 'gold coats' of 17th century origin, denoting

Left to right, from top: The aiguillettes of the Silver Stick in Waiting.

The Gold Stick.

The red plume and the blue tunic of The Blues and Royals.

The kettledrums of The Blues and Royals with drum banners fitted.

The Silver Stick.

A Trumpeter's Gold Coat with Iraq medal and trumpet with banner fitted.

The ivory plume and red tunic of The Life Guards.

The kettledrums of The Life Guards.

them as State musicians. The kettledrums of both Regiments are made of silver. The Life Guards have two sets presented by King William IV in 1831 to the 1st & 2nd Life Guards; The Blues and Royals' kettledrums were presented to The Blues by King George III in 1805. Both the kettledrums and the trumpets are draped with embroidered silk banners bearing the royal coat-of-arms.

There are still a number of Household Cavalrymen who served in the Mounted Regiment at the old Knightsbridge Barracks immediately after World War II, before it was replaced by Sir Basil Spence's unloved concrete and brick edifice in 1972. One stalwart survivor of that era is John Cowdery, who enlisted in the Royal Horse Guards in 1949, and did several tours of duty at the old Knightsbridge Barracks:

The barrack rooms, which were over the stables, were long and thin with a row of beds down each side and a round black coke stove at the far end. The nearer your bed was to the stove the warmer you were – but you also had to endure the coke fumes…
at night you could hear two things, the roar of the traffic on South Carriage Drive and the sound of horses chaffing and stamping in the stables below.

John remembers performing the King's Life Guard in khaki uniform, the finery of State Kit having been packed away at the start of the war. He also remembers that when they began using it again, everyone had forgotten the secret of how to clean and take care of it, and it was many years before standards crept back up to where they had once been. In a long and distinguished career, John also served with his Regiment in Windsor, at Herford in Germany and twice in Cyprus. John ended his military service as Garrison Sergeant Major of 1BR Corps in Germany.

The Eagle captured at Waterloo from the 105th French Infantry Regiment, and still worn on the uniforms of The Blues and Royals today.

Historic uniforms, paintings and silver from the collection on display in the Household Cavalry Museum, Horse Guards Parade, Whitehall.

Soldiers of 'The Blues' waiting to be inspected outside the old Knightsbridge Barracks.

The Definite Article

The two Regiments of Household Cavalry share the unique honour of being allowed to capitalise the definite article in their names. For The Life Guards this acknowledges that they were formed from two separate regiments: the 1st and 2nd Life Guards. Similarly, when the Blues (Royal Horse Guards) and the Royals (1st Dragoons) amalgamated in 1969 the same privilege was extended.

Left: *The Drum Horse* by the world-famous equestrian artist Sir Alfred Munnings, RA.

Below: The 1857 picture by I. Dickenson of the Officers of the 1st Life Guards reclining in their various uniforms.

In addition to the priceless silver kettledrums and trumpets, both Regiments have a fine collection of silver and paintings held in the Officers' and the Warrant Officers and NCOs' Messes, with new pieces joining the collection in most years. For many years, the Household Cavalry's extensive historical collection and archives were stored and displayed in a small museum within Combermere Barracks, Windsor. In 2007, the collection was moved to the Horse Guards building in Whitehall, London, where a new Household Cavalry Museum was created within William Kent's finely vaulted stables constructed in 1751.

Right: One of the most famous pieces of silver in the Regiment depicts the 'Moonlight Charge' of the Household Cavalry against the Egyptians at Kassassin.

Following page: 'More polish required!' Squadron Corporal Major 'Paddy' Ireland inspects The Blues and Royals as part of the build-up to another busy State Ceremonial season. Each man has his uniform individually fitted to him by the Regiment's Saddlers, Tailors and Armourer, seen here in tow. Neither the process nor the uniforms have changed for hundreds of years.

CHAPTER 4

Earning The Queen's Shilling

In former times, when every cavalry regiment of the British Army was horsed, there was a saying that ruled a regiment's life: 'First the horses, then the soldiers and only then the officers.' That axiom held true for many years, although there is now much greater emphasis on the needs of our soldiers than in days gone by.

Horses are, by their very nature, time intensive and require constant care and attention. The Mounted Regiment has an exacting daily routine which must be maintained 365 days a year. In winter and summer, come rain or shine – and usually long before most Londoners are awake – the Household Cavalry Mounted Regiment's day starts at 0530 hrs with reveille and then morning stables.

We exercise the horses on the streets of London between 0700-0800 hrs each day, in a practice known as a Watering Order. This relates to times past when the horses would be watered together on their return from exercise. Dressed in khaki and generally with each soldier riding one horse and leading another, the Household Cavalry ventures forth as they have for centuries onto the streets of Chelsea, Knightsbridge, Kensington, Mayfair and even as far as Piccadilly Circus and Battersea. Residents and motorists are familiar with the early morning sound of hooves on tarmac, although tourists are a little more surprised by the sight if they are up and about!

Left: 'The beginning of a long day.' Mucking out the horses in Two Troop, The Life Guards Mounted Squadron stables.

Every day The Life Guards or The Blues and Royals prepare for the Queen's Life Guard, a Public Duty that dates back to the Restoration of the Monarchy in 1660, when one or more Troops of Horse Guards were stationed at Horse Guards to guard the front gate of the principal royal residence, which was then the Palace of Whitehall. They also provided the monarch with a mounted bodyguard whenever he or she left the palace, so the guard was as much as 100 strong.

Despite the main royal residence moving first to St James's Palace in 1698 and then, in the early 19th century, to Buckingham Palace, the King's or Queen's Life Guard has remained at Horse Guards to guard the main or official entrance to the sovereign's residence.

The Life Guards and The Blues and Royals perform the duty on alternate days to effect the Changing of the Queen's Life Guard, which starts at 11 o'clock (10 o'clock on Sundays) daily. The ceremony is held on Horse Guards Parade with the Old and New Guards facing each other to exchange duties.

The Queen's Life Guard routinely comprises 12 soldiers, 2 Non-Commissioned Officers (or NCOs) and 10 Troopers, and is popularly known as a 'Short Guard'. If The Queen is resident in London, the addition of an Officer ('the Captain of the Queen's Life Guard'), a Warrant Officer carrying a Standard, and a Trumpeter turns it into a 'Long Guard'. The guard is then 'made-up' or 'made-down' according to The Queen's movements. One story from previous years entails an impatient Captain of the Queen's Life Guard telephoning Buckingham Palace repeatedly to confirm whether Her Majesty had indeed departed for the weekend, only to hear an instantly recognisable voice in the background say, "Tell him that I will leave when I am good and ready!"

The requirement to furnish an on-going and off-coming Queen's Life Guard every day of the year, even on Christmas Day, dominates the daily routine at Hyde Park Barracks. Aside from the large parades, soldiers will perform about 6 or 7 of these 24-hour guard duties every month, with another 24 hours spent in preparation for the kit inspection. Long hours of equipment cleaning and maintenance, with everything to be presented to the highest possible standard, makes for a gruelling and repetitive routine that is not always visible to the tourists who flock to Horse Guards. Next time you are in Whitehall and see a young Household Cavalry soldier on duty, take time to reflect that he has just spent about 8 hours polishing his boots. It is also worth remembering that the men on duty in Whitehall may only recently have been operating armoured vehicles in Afghanistan, or parachuting in their airborne role.

Throughout the year the horses require constant care and attention. The wear and tear inflicted on horses' hooves and shoes by the hard London streets mean that the forge and Regimental Farriers are kept busy throughout the day. The horses are shod on average every 3 to 4 weeks. Veterinary care is provided by the Regimental Veterinary Officer in the Sick Lines, with soldiers' injuries cared for by the Regimental Surgeon. Both the Veterinary Officer and Surgeon wear Household Cavalry uniform, and regularly parade mounted with the Regiment.

'Green Light.' Capt Hopkinson and WO2 Newell use their best map-reading skills to negotiate the morning traffic of Piccadilly on a Watering Order. Watering Orders were originally undertaken to water the horses from surrounding troughs before piped water was available in the Barracks.

Captain Anton Wallis and Eliza cut a dash through the morning rush hour.

'Breakfast Time.' LCpl Shutt turns in his horse after Watering Order.

Trooper Robinson shares out the carrots and prepares for 'Feed Away'. The horses are always given their food before the soldiers eat theirs. This reinforces the principles of good animal husbandry and remembers the old saying, 'Your horse, your kit, yourself.'

LCpl Capes puts the finishing touches to his boots the evening before a parade.

'The Jackboot Waddle.' Dismounted Troopers Mardon, Bell and Morrison are careful not to crack the wax on their boots after many hours of work. By strutting their stuff in this way they may look rather strange, but ensure they save many hours of work repairing damage.

Above left: Inclement weather. During heavy rain, the Four O'Clock Inspection is carried out in the comparative privacy of the stable archway. In the summer, there can be up to 200 tourists and as many lenses. Mistakes at that range are hard to hide. ***Above***: 'Nobody move!' Two hours standing in the kit can be a real challenge. ***Left***: The cleanest men have the privilege of being mounted on guard and are called 'Boxmen' after the sentry boxes from which they look out onto Whitehall.

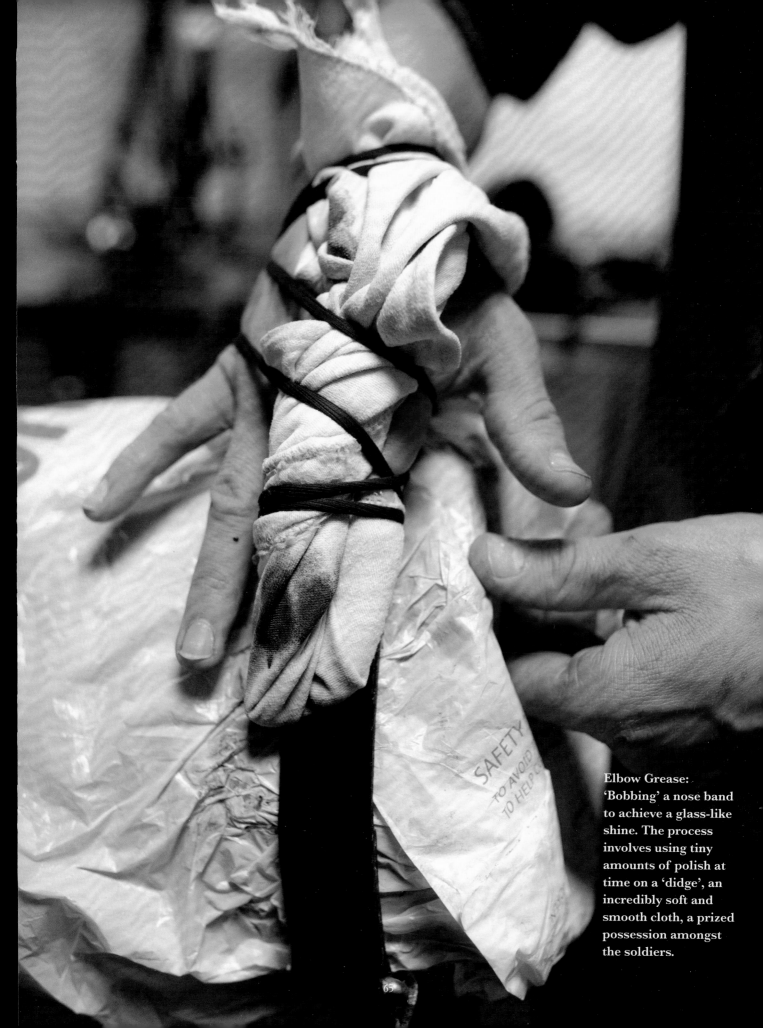

Elbow Grease: 'Bobbing' a nose band to achieve a glass-like shine. The process involves using tiny amounts of polish at time on a 'didge', an incredibly soft and smooth cloth, a prized possession amongst the soldiers.

'Tinning in', the technique of using
a tin lid to force layers of polish into
the leather, thus creating a deeper
shine. A horse's kit can take up to
six hours to complete properly.

Top: 'Hammer and tongs.' The Farrier Major shapes a shoe in the forge. The horses' shoes are bought in various sizes but are individually shaped by the Farriers to each hoof. The Farriers have the ability to make all types of horse shoes simply from working bar metal. The standard of farriery is exemplary. ***Bottom left***: LCoH Wenham is one of the Regiment's saddlers who make, fit and maintain every piece of kit that sits on a horse and many that are worn by the soldiers. ***Bottom right***: In a painless process for the horse, the hot shoe is fitted to the hoof.

Fitness is at the basis of what we do, so regular Physical Training is undertaken.

'Stillness in the Snow.' The Old Guard
wait to be relieved on Horse Guards
Parade, Whitehall. The men remain
rigid, but the horses take the opportunity
to look around at their newly blanketed
surroundings.

71

Above: The Orderly Officer of the day, Captain Anton Wallis, rides down the Mall to Horse Guards to perform the Four O'Clock Inspection of the Queen's Life Guard. ***Opposite page***: The 1902 Pattern Military Saddle is specifically designed to distribute the weight of a uniformed man evenly across the horse and has not fundamentally changed in 400 years.

CHAPTER 5

Pomp & Circumstance

The day-to-day routine at Hyde Park Barracks, and the unique privilege of performing the daily Queen's Life Guard, represent just a few of the elements that make up our overall commitment. There are a whole range of very public State Ceremonial duties for which we are responsible. These are generally fixed in the annual ceremonial calendar and are the points around which training revolves. The busiest period in May and June each year is popularly referred to as the 'Silly Season' by the soldiers. It normally opens and closes with a State Visit by a foreign Head of State, with the State Opening of Parliament, The Queen's Birthday Parade (or Trooping the Colour) and the Garter Service falling in between. State Banquets, Investitures and Step-lining Parties for foreign dignitaries fill much of the time left, with one-off events such as a Royal Wedding providing a welcome variation to our routine.

We are often asked why, in the 21st century, we still carry out Ceremonial duties. The City of London ceremonial handbook puts it neatly:

Ceremonies are not idle forms or shows put on merely for entertainment; they ensure that things are done with dignity and in good order.

Left: The end is in sight. Lining the route for the Garter Procession and Service which takes place at Windsor Castle at the end of the State Ceremonial season. The Order of the Garter is the senior and oldest British Order of Chivalry, founded by Edward III in 1348.

But it is much more than that. We exist to contribute to the dignity of the State and, in doing so, we reinforce the link between the Armed Forces and the Sovereign. These parades are recognised (and iconic) symbols of the United Kingdom and form a distinctive part of the 'fabric of the Nation'. For a small country with global interests, State Ceremonial duties are also a powerful symbol of our national culture and military heritage – and, thereby, are a considerable instrument of soft power. We rightly have a world-wide reputation for our ceremonial displays and we are the envy of many countries who use our ceremonial soldiers and formations as a model for their own.

There are generally two State Visits a year made to the UK by visiting Heads of State. These can take place either in London or Windsor and, very occasionally, in Edinburgh. It falls to the Household Cavalry to provide a Sovereign's Escort for these visits, the function of which is to provide immediate close protection to the carriages and Royal occupants being escorted.

For larger State Ceremonial parades, we will be organised into 'divisions', blocks of 24 soldiers and horses riding four abreast, with the officer riding front left. A 'March-Out' for the Mounted Regiment could include as many as six mounted divisions, which is approximately 180 men and horses including Standard Parties, the command element, and smaller escorts. We also provide all the horses for the two Household Cavalry Mounted Bands (the Band of The Life Guards and the Band of The Blues & Royals).

A Sovereign's Escort consists of four divisions, drawn equally from The Life Guards and The Blues and Royals. Each division is commanded by an Officer, with two divisions leading the carriage procession and two bringing up the rear. The Escort is commanded by the 'Field Officer of the Escort' and an 'Escort Commander', who deputises at certain points during the parade. There is always at least one Standard and sometimes two, at the centre of the parade party. The Farriers bring up the rear.

In the past, The Queen's guests were met at Victoria railway station and travelled in a carriage procession through the streets of London to Buckingham Palace. However, because of

traffic congestion and security issues, the processional route now starts on Horse Guards and travels up The Mall to Buckingham Palace. In Windsor, by contrast, visiting Heads of State are usually met at Windsor Riverside station and proceed through the town to Windsor Castle via the Long Walk, altogether a much longer journey.

The date of the State Opening of Parliament is generally determined by the date of a General Election and then held annually thereafter for the life of that Parliament. In addition to providing a

Sovereign's Escort to escort The Queen from Buckingham Palace to the Palace of Westminster and back again, the Regiment also provides a Regalia Escort to accompany the Crown Regalia, and a dismounted Staircase Lining Party on the Norman Porch stairs near the Sovereign's Entrance.

Immediately following The Queen's Birthday Parade in mid-June, and acting as the unofficial end to the ceremonial season, the Garter Knights, including The Queen and many other members of the Royal Family, walk from Windsor Castle to St George's Chapel for a service of dedication. The route is lined by nearly 100 of our dismounted soldiers who stand at attention for an hour in the heat, waiting for the end of the service. There is always a collective sigh of relief as we board the coaches to return to Knightsbridge, safe in the knowledge that we have survived another 'Silly Season'.

Top: 'All eyes on one man.' The Dismount takes place on the Regimental Parade Square. All actions go off the timings of the right-hand man.
Above: 'Upstairs Downstairs.' The Blues and Royals are stabled on the level above The Life Guards: an arrangement designed by Sir Basil Spence.

Restless heads in the crisp morning air. Immaculately dressed-off and ready for their inspection before the city wakes. Early Morning Rehearsals are conducted at about 5am, meaning that reveille for soldiers and horses is about 2am. The early start means that the parade can be practised without causing too much traffic disruption.

Having handed over the Sovereign's Standard to the Corporal Major for
the duration of the parade, the Standard Bearers, LCpl Davidson, LCoH
Tirimaidoka and CoH Mowatt, salute our most treasured and protected symbol
of identity.

Top: 'Just a trim, please.' Trooper Corbett tidies up the plume of LCpl Marsden during the Squadron kit inspection. ***Above***: The drawing of swords is as regimented as one would expect! Every man follows the exact timings of the Field Officer.

Within the quadrangle of Windsor Castle, and having delivered The Queen after the Sovereign's Escort, the Rank Past takes place. Here The Queen can individually look over each of her men and horses.

A Double-Standard Sovereign's Escort for a State Visit. Here The President of Turkey accompanies The Queen to Buckingham Palace following his Royal welcome in November 2011. This Escort is the highest honour that the Nation bestows on a visiting Head of State.

Above: Leaving St George's Chapel, Windsor, after the Garter Service. Here we line the route on one of our few dismounted parades, and the one that marks the end of the 'Silly Season'.

Opposite page: 'Returning Swords.' With sometimes over 200 horses on the parade square at one time, the returning of swords and dismount is a strictly choreographed routine which ensures that the number of collisions and stabbings are kept to a minimum!

The Adjutant, Captain Roly Spiller, is responsible for inspecting the Regiment before any rehearsals. If someone has not met the high standards required, they will be replaced on parade by the 'Waiting Man'.

The Rank Past during The Queen's Birthday Parade is done in a 'Divisional Frontage' of twelve abreast and provides the best opportunity for The Queen to review her troops.

This page top: 'Not as easy as it looks.' The Staircase Party descends the steps at the Sovereign's entrance at the Palace of Westminster. *Bottom*: For state occasions such as this visit by President Barack Obama, seen here with His Royal Highness the Duke of Edinburgh, perfection is essential.

Opposite top left: 'An eye for detail.' The Staircase Party is inspected on the parade square in barracks. *Top right*: The dummy standards await collection by the Squadron Corporals Major. The real Standards are presented by The Queen but are not used on rehearsals. *Bottom*: Preparations for the Staircase Party culminate in a khaki rehearsal in which only key parts of the ceremonial uniform are worn.

The Blues and Royals emerge into the gloom and rain before Squadron Drills.

The Life Guards trot down Whitehall during an Early Morning Rehearsal.

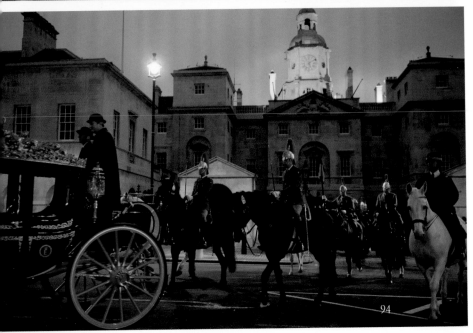

The Queen's Carriage passes through Horse Guards Arch in the early dawn. The arch is the historical entrance to the Royal residences and is where the Queen's Life Guard stands on duty all year round.

94

'Our bodies are here but our minds are thinking of breakfast.' After a long and wet Regimental Drills session Major Simon Deverell, the Field Officer, leads the damp column of men and horses home.

The Queen passes through Horse Guards en route to the State Opening of Parliament. The Officer's sword and the Standard must be dipped as the front wheel of the carriage passes.

Soldiers of the Queen's Life Guard spend 24 hours on duty at Horse Guards. The men and horses live in situ for the duration of their guard.

This page top and middle: Soldiers in the stables. ***Bottom***: LCpl Hirst and Corporal Major Gibson watch the State Opening of Parliament from the Guardroom.

Opposite: Horse Guards Arch is too narrow for four abreast. Here the third man, having dropped back for the arch, regains his position.

The Queen's Life Guard is passed by the third division of the Sovereign's Escort as the carriage turns onto Whitehall.

Resplendent in her 60th year of service to the Nation, The Queen is escorted to address both Houses during the State Opening of Parliament.

The Life Guards lead the carriage home.

'Halfway there.' The Queen's carriage arrives on time at The Palace of Westminster and disappears into The Sovereign's Entrance. Meanwhile Numbers One and Two Division of the Escort form up whilst Three and Four Division close the gap.

CHAPTER 6

Trooping the Colour

Of all the State Ceremonial occasions in the diary of the Household Cavalry Mounted Regiment, the annual parade to mark the official birthday of Her Majesty The Queen is the one best known to the public. Strictly speaking, The Queen's Birthday Parade (or 'Trooping the Colour' as most know it) is a Foot Guards parade, and our role is to provide a Sovereign's Escort, accompanied by the Mounted Bands, to escort Her Majesty to and from Buckingham Palace.

Rehearsals for the parade start three weeks before, with an Early Morning Rehearsal (otherwise known as the String Band Rehearsal) purely for the mounted troops, followed by two formal rehearsals for all participants on the two preceding Saturdays. These are known as the Major General's Review and the Colonel's Review.

The Early Morning Rehearsal is something of a Mounted Regiment tradition and ensures we have completed our rehearsal and are clear of the busy London streets before the rush hour starts. The troops normally start with a 0230 hrs reveille and early morning stables, with soldiers mounted and ready to depart by 0500 hrs. It is a surreal sight to watch 200 soldiers mount up and leave the barracks to conduct a full rehearsal in the pitch dark before the rest of London has woken up. A hearty breakfast after we return at around 0700 hrs sets us up for the remainder of the working day, although with many bleary eyes around in certain departments!

On the day of The Queen's Birthday Parade itself, horses and soldiers are again up early to prepare for the parade. From the barracks we ride to Buckingham Palace, where we meet up with The Queen's carriage, and provide an escort to Horse Guards Parade. Over the years, the Household Cavalry's participation in the parade has increased so that, once the chosen Foot Guard battalion's Colour has been 'trooped', our Mounted Bands take over the music, and the four divisions of the Sovereign's Escort walk and trot past our Colonel-in-Chief. It is a proud moment for the young soldiers who have never experienced it, and even for those old sweats who have seen it many times before, it sends a tingle down the spine.

Once completed, the Mounted Bands and the Sovereign's Escort head the procession back to Buckingham Palace, before a 'Rank Past' Her Majesty and the return to Hyde Park Barracks. For the soldiers and horses it is an exhausting parade as most of us will be in the saddle for nearly 4 hours, often in the blazing sun. The sense of relief as we remove our state helmets and sweat-soaked tunics after the parade is palpable. As always after a parade, our focus is on ensuring the horses are fed, watered, bedded down and comfortable, before we make the most of the rest of the weekend.

Previous page: Major Nana Twumasi-Ankrah gives an 'eyes right' on The Queen's Birthday Parade.

Left: Her Majesty returns to Buckingham Palace from Horse Guards Parade escorted now by the Royal Colonels of the Household Division.

Opposite top: "Number 3 Division, Royal Salute, eyes right!" Paying compliments to Her Majesty. The Divisions must maintain a precisely straight line. Holding the 'dressing', easy enough on your feet, becomes increasingly difficult on horses and at speed. *Bottom*: Garrison Sergeant Major WO1 Mott and the Silver Stick, Colonel Stuart Cowen, discuss the parade.

A Mounted Band accompanies the Queen's Life Guard. This is done to prepare the horses and musicians alike for Trooping the Colour.

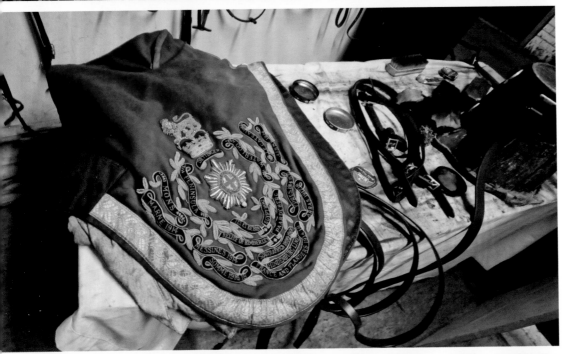

A Drum Horse shabraque.

The Mounted Band retires away from the camera during a rehearsal. The band has to have the most sedate of all our horses as while they are playing they have limited steering capabilities!

SCpl Griffiths seeks the counsel of the Garrison Sergeant Major, a man who has a wealth of experience in all things Ceremonial.

Squadron Corporal Major Gibson dips the Dummy Standard to the dais. On the day, The Queen, who now has 60 years of experience, can identify the slightest mistake at a distance. Perfection is imperative!

With the Mall
bedecked with Union
Flags, the parade is
'Uniquely British'
and encapsulates
what we do best.

111

The Rank Past on The Queen's Birthday
Parade. The Divisions spread out until
they are twelve abreast and as visible as
possible for our Colonel-in-Chief.

Their Royal Highnesses Prince Henry of Wales, The Duchess of Cornwall, and The Duchess of Cambridge at The Queen's Birthday Parade 2011. It was the first time The Duchess of Cambridge had attended the parade in an official capacity.

Her Majesty The Queen and The Duke of Edinburgh mount the dais outside Buckingham Palace, as the Regiment positions itself to Rank Past for the final time before heading home.

CHAPTER 7

On the Front Line

Every Household Cavalry soldier is first and foremost a fighting soldier. The troops you see participating in ceremonial parades are fully trained, operational troops. Soldiers and officers of the Household Cavalry are tough, resourceful and proud of their Regiment's operational heritage. All Household Cavalrymen regularly rotate between ceremonial duties in London and front-line soldiering with the Household Cavalry Regiment based in Windsor.

This commitment to two roles is perhaps best illustrated by the number of bravery awards and campaign medals which can be seen worn every day by the Household Cavalrymen deployed on Public Duties. However, the medals don't tell the whole story, which is best related by the men themselves.

Comrades-in-arms – Captain Roly Spiller and Corporal of Horse Anthony Todd

It was on Op HERRICK 8 in 2008 that Captain Roly Spiller, currently the Adjutant of the Mounted Regiment, and Corporal of Horse Anthony Todd, of The Life Guards, found themselves involved in the same fatal IED (Improvised Explosive Device) incident.

Left: 'Heading home.' After a long and strenuous tour of Helmand Province, one of the Scimitar vehicles of 'A' Squadron HCR returns to Camp Bastion flying the Household Division colours and the Union Flag.

Roly Spiller, who had chosen an Army career because he "didn't want to spend the best years of my life moving numbers around a screen" tells the story:

I was Assault Troop Leader on that tour. The Troop's job was to clear vehicle routes of IEDs and provide real punch if we came into contact with the insurgents. Our first big operation was to head a convoy west from Musa Qala into the desert, then swing north through the mountains and re-emerge to the east of Musa Qala at Kariz deh Baba where the insurgents were using an extensive underground canal network for hardware storage and as a base for smuggling.

My Spartan was heading up the convoy and, at a certain point on the march, we had to clear a route across a series of very steep wadis. We were on a well-used track but it was unsuitable for the logistics vehicles, so I ordered my vehicle off the track. Turning a corner, the rear of the Spartan clipped either an IED or a Russian legacy mine, which detonated and the blast hit the side of our vehicle. I was half out of the turret at the time and the blast wrapped itself around me, bent my GPMG into a 90 degree angle, ripped the headset from under my helmet and hurled the vehicle's radio set into my left side.

To my surprise, at that moment, I felt absolutely OK. My colleagues had fared less well. Sadly, Trooper Babakobau was clearly dead; our Afghan interpreter had been blown through the roof and was trapped between the mortar plates; my driver, Trooper Baker, was wedged in his hatch, temporarily blinded and in severe pain from a smashed pelvis – and our radio operator, Lance Corporal of Horse Todd had been thrown 30 feet away from the vehicle, apparently without a scratch.

Anthony Todd, a combat veteran who started his Army career in the Green Howards, and had already undertaken operational tours as an infantryman in Bosnia, Northern Ireland and Afghanistan, takes up the story:

I was in the forward turret of the vehicle and, when the blast hit, I was leaning out of it giving instructions to our driver, Baker. I was conscious of the explosion and then, moments later, of looking back at the vehicle from a distance of about thirty feet. I know I was blasted from one position to the other, but I have no memory of it. The next thing I knew, Mr Spiller was yelling at me not to move as I might have been in a minefield. That's when you reap the benefit of drill: even though I was dazed and confused, I froze on the spot.

The crew in the lead vehicle were very quick at clearing a path to me. They seemed to get to me in only a matter of a few minutes but whilst they were doing

'Train hard and fight easy.' Members of 'D' Squadron HCR exercise on Salisbury Plain whilst preparing for operations in Afghanistan.

CoH Todd, LCoH
Glasgow, LCpl John
and Captain Spiller
in the stables at Horse
Guards. The Household
Cavalry Museum is
directly adjacent to these
stables and has only glass
separating the two,
meaning that the public
can see the workings of
the stables.

so I was looking at my vehicle. There was quite a lot of activity on it, so I assumed that everyone was all right. It was only when I got back to the lead vehicle and had lit-up that I started to realise that everything was very much not alright – and the extent became clear in the Chinook that took us to Camp Bastion. Mr Spiller was clearly in a lot of pain, Baba was lying dead on a stretcher next to me, Baker was unconscious and our Afghan interpreter looked more than half dead, although he kept saying over and over again 'F*** the Taliban!'.

Because I had nothing worse than a bit of concussion, I was soon back on duty and Mr Spiller was back after three months. Baker and our Afghan interpreter also survived, but sadly there was nothing to be done for Baba from the moment the IED hit us.

The 'war stories' only paint part of the picture of the very diverse collection of characters who make up the Household Cavalry. Two in particular show how far we cast our recruiting net.

Bombs, bullets and a President – Lance Corporal of Horse Jason Glasgow and Lance Corporal Denton John

Jason Glasgow is, by any standard, an unusual Household Cavalryman. Born in Trinidad, as a young man he joined the Trinidad and Tobago Regiment, in which he served for two and a half years, rising to the rank of Lance Corporal.

However, in search of broader horizons, he moved to the USA where, after a couple of years on civvy street, he applied to join the US Marine Corps. But, at the last minute, he changed his mind.

I was keen to get back into uniform. My sister was living abroad and she suggested that, instead of the US Marines, I should look at the British Army, which I did on-line. I liked what I saw, so I filled out the application and was almost immediately accepted. I'd never been to England before but, a few weeks later, I found myself at a Recruiting Centre in Manchester. My original idea was to join either the Intelligence Corps or the Paras, but an old injury in my ankle put paid to that – so instead I joined the Household Cavalry and I don't regret that decision for an instant.

After I had trained as a driver at Bovington, I joined 'D' Squadron in Windsor and soon found myself driving a Spartan in Afghanistan as part of our deployment on Op HERRICK 4 in 2006. It was a crazy time and the experience really changed me. The public was focussed on Iraq and had no idea what was going on in Afghanistan; but we were busy, very busy. My first experience of the reality of the war there was when, inbound to Musa Qala to resupply the pathfinders, my Spartan was destroyed by a Russian legacy mine. We were lucky as, although I sustained burns to my left arm and took some shrapnel in my chin, which is still there, we were otherwise unharmed. The next day we weren't so lucky. I was on my feet with a mortar helping to suppress the insurgents' fire when Mr Johnson's Spartan was taken out by an IED. He was killed and Martyn Compton was very badly burned – his only recognisable features as we loaded him onto the Chinook were his eyes.

Since then I've done three more operational tours – Op TELIC 10 in Basra, then Op HERRICKs 10 and 11. In the late summer last year I was given a choice of my next posting: as a training troop NCO at Bovington or on the horses at Knightsbridge. Well, with the Olympics and the Jubilee scheduled for 2012, it seemed to me that the chance to be part of two historic occasions was too good to miss, so I opted for Knightsbridge. I had hardly ever ridden before I joined the Khaki Ride last September, but I managed not to get binned until almost the last day of the Ride.

The Mounted Regiment is very different to Windsor, but the spirit is the same. In fact, the only thing that I don't like about Knightsbridge…is horses that kick!

Denton John is reasonably confident that he is the only US citizen currently serving in the British Army – and certainly the only one in the Household Cavalry – a fact that came home to him when, in May 2011 during the State Visit of President Obama, he found himself shaking the President's hand whilst on a Staircase Lining Party.

It was a pretty surreal experience for both of us, I think. The first black American President and the first black American Household Cavalryman saying 'hello' in London with Her Majesty The Queen looking on.

The journey from New York City to that moment was strange enough and started in 2007 when I took a gap year in Grenada after High School in New York. I had been bumming around in Grenada for a few months doing odd jobs, including bar tending and working on construction sites, when my uncle suggested that I think about joining the army – the British Army. Well, because I was born in Grenada I have dual citizenship, so I took the preliminary tests on-line, passed them and six months later I was on the square at Pirbright.

One Troop, 'A' Squadron HCR, shadowed by their Jackal vehicles, deploy on foot for a patrol of Babaji in Helmand Province. LCpl Deavall (left) and LCoH O'Leary (centre) have recently served at the Mounted Regiment.

I had done a lot of homework before I arrived in England and I knew that I wanted to be a Household Cavalryman, because it was the best – and it offered 'the best of both worlds' – although I assumed that I would start on the armoured reconnaissance side. But no, on completion of Phase 1 training, I found myself mucking out horses at Windsor.

Before I joined the Khaki Ride, the only horses I had ever seen were on television and I can tell you that they are pretty scary creatures when you first get up close. But I survived, I passed out of the Kit Ride in October 2009 and, after only a short time at Knightsbridge, I was put on the recruiting team and spent most of 2010 touring the UK. Before I arrived at Pirbright I had never been on this side of the Atlantic so it was a great way to get to know this country.

I was posted back to Knightsbridge just in time for Major General's inspection in March 2011 and ever since then it seems to have been non-stop. President Obama's State Visit was followed by the Royal Wedding, which I thought was going to be just another Escort, but the media descended on Knightsbridge, someone told them I was an American and I found myself the focus of their attention. I had to ride down to a spot outside Buckingham Palace where I was interviewed from on top of my horse surrounded by journalists, TV cameras and tourists. It was awesome.

Now we're getting ready for this year's ceremonial season that will end with the Diamond Jubilee Escort. It's hard to believe that I'm a part of it all and the folks back in New York are really impressed! But when it's all over, I want to be posted to Windsor and hopefully get in an Op HERRICK tour before that's all over. Then? Well – I'll see.

Meanwhile, I will continue to be the only Household Cavalryman to celebrate the 4th July – although I'm trying to educate my mates – and I'm still wondering if it was deliberate or just an accident that I got my first promotion on Thanksgiving Day.

As these stories amply illustrate, over the past two decades our soldiers have been deployed to fight in virtually every conflict, most notably in Bosnia, Kosovo, Iraq and Afghanistan. Training for the Regiment's deployment in the armoured reconnaissance role takes place at Windsor and on training areas as far away as the central plains of Canada.

Household Cavalrymen are also regularly deployed with other units including the Parachute Regiment, Special Forces, and the Army Air Corps. The maroon beret, which is only worn by parachute-qualified soldiers, and 'wings' denoting parachutists, aviators and SAS, are a common sight.

With wet legs from patrolling the Green Zone, a 'D' Squadron patrol pushes out into the heat and dust of the village of Hazrat, east of Gereshk in Helmand Province.

1. LCoH Capp takes advantage of the shade during a hot foot-patrol in Helmand. The ever-present threat of Improvised Explosive Devices is evident from the Vallon Mine detector at his side. *2*. The silhouetted soldier at sunset. *3*. The troop team photograph at the end of their tour. *4*. A 'D' Squadron Jackal vehicle deployed as part of 16 Air Assault Brigade with the Parachute Regiment. *5*. A Troop Leaguer, which is a defensive formation employed by vehicles at night as a protective measure. *6*. 'Progress being made.' Dawn Patrol.

Captain Simon Lukas, shadowed by interpreters and members of the Afghan Security Forces, holds a Shura, or meeting with elders to discuss local issues.

A foot-patrol cautiously crosses a field of opium poppies in Nahr e Seraj North, Helmand Province.

Two Troop of 'A' Squadron HCR strike a pose outside a newly constructed Patrol Base having seized control of the Bolan Desert from insurgents during Operation Moshtarak 2010.

131

WOI Shaun Fry MC, the Regimental Corporal Major of the Household Cavalry Regiment, has no doubts about the Regiment or his role in it:

The Household Cavalry is unique, for it combines the very high standards of the Foot Guards with the skills of the Royal Armoured Corps. My job is to keep everyone in line with those standards. If we let them slip, we become just like everyone else.

With 22 years' service that includes the first Gulf War, Northern Ireland, Bosnia, Iraq and three tours to date in Afghanistan, Shaun Fry leads by example, as is evidenced by his Military Cross. This rare medal is awarded only for "an act or acts of exemplary gallantry during active operations against the enemy on land."

In 2006, Shaun, then a Corporal of Horse, was a Forward Air Controller attached to 'A' Company, 3 Para in Helmand Province. Early on in the tour, 'A' Company conducted a cordon and search of an insurgents' compound in Nowzad. From the moment of landing from the Chinook helicopters, the British troops were subjected to heavy fire from the insurgents which lasted for six hours. Eventually, the order to withdraw was given. In order to ensure continued air support to cover the extraction, Shaun Fry as the FAC was the last man out. As he ran from cover to the helicopter, his last act was to call down an A-10 air strike on his own position.

Several months later, and still attached to 'A' Company, 3 Para, Shaun was part of an operation to extract a high-ranking Afghan policeman from a police compound, located in the heart of one of the most lawless areas of Afghanistan, the Sangin valley. 'A' Company, equipped only with what they were carrying, got the policeman out without a fight and were ordered to 'hold and stay'. For a week all was peaceful, then the insurgents struck back.

The assault lasted for two weeks, during which time there was no resupply for the beleaguered Paras. Shaun and his FSG team had positioned themselves on top of a derelict tower just outside the police compound. The tower was targeted by the insurgents and struck by a 107 mm rocket, during which casualties were sustained, including Shaun. However, having got himself patched-up in the compound by medics, Shaun returned to the tower and directed a B-1 Bomber strike on the insurgents, which resulted in their withdrawal and the safe extraction of the defenders.

These two acts of calculated gallantry earned Shaun the Military Cross.

Opposite: Regimental Quartermaster Corporal 'Sizzler' Fry MC.

CHAPTER 8

Regimental Training

Whilst the armoured reconnaissance role requires weeks of training, sharing the Canadian prairie with gophers and rattlesnakes, and Salisbury Plain with muntjacs and mud, training for the mounted role is a more domestic affair.

It starts at the Training Wing at Combermere Barracks, Windsor, where our new recruits are taught the basic equitation skills that will enable them to become Mounted Dutymen. Most of them will never have sat on a horse before, and they need to embrace their fears quickly as they are introduced on their second day to a ton of biting, kicking 'Cavalry Black'!

Novices are organised into 'rides' which, over the training cycle, progress from 'Khaki' in Windsor to 'Kit' rides in London. The inevitable falls that occur on the recruit rides are cushioned slightly by the soft surfaces of the indoor and outdoor riding schools. But it is not just pride that suffers, and an unofficial sweepstake ensures that those who fall off most are also the most popular in the pub!

All the training is done by the Riding Staff, twelve expert instructors led by the Riding Master, who are responsible for training not just the novice riders, but also the horses from purchase, through breaking and schooling, to the finished article on parade.

At the Training Wing, our recruits also learn about stable and horse management including mucking out, feeding, grooming and basic veterinary skills. Once these skills have been taught, the trainees learn the fundamentals of military equitation and take part in mounted drills. During Kit Ride our trainee Mounted Dutymen have to be fitted with full State Kit, before learning to clean and polish it, and lastly learning to ride in it. Weighing up to six stone and worn for as long as eight hours at a time, the discomforts of wearing State Kit when in the saddle for protracted periods cannot be overemphasised. There is a joke that if the Quartermaster asks a new soldier whether his state helmet fits comfortably, an affirmative answer will result in it being swapped for another which is far less comfortable. The wise head of the Quartermaster knows that a 'comfortable' helmet is likely to move around on parade in a sloppy manner!

The metal armour plates (cuirasses) were once intended to stop sword slashes and musket balls. Since 1821, they have been highly polished as a symbol of our role as Heavy Cavalry. A white 'cartouche belt' is worn over the cuirasses like a bandolier. The sword is the 1892 pattern and saw action in the Boer War. The jackboots are perhaps the most infamous bits of kit. These are waxed hard and have many layers of polish applied. Far shinier and more durable than any patent leather, they are a source of fevered competition between soldiers.

For three weeks every summer, the Regiment leaves London and deploys to a training area in Norfolk to develop our riding skills and rehearse State Ceremonial events. We also undergo 'green' training to keep our military skills alive. Bodney Camp near Thetford is the normal location, and in the more relaxed atmosphere of 'Summer Camp', our men and horses hone their equitation and military skills, as well as learning new ones such as tent-pegging and skill-at-arms. There is also time to ride the horses on the wide open Norfolk beaches at Holkham. At the end of Regimental Training, we stage an Open Weekend to which we invite people from across the country to view the stables, meet the horses and enjoy our equestrian performances.

Right: Faces of exhaustion at the end of a gruelling three and a half mile stretcher race. **Previous page**: 'Honing our skills.' Horses and riders practise before the Regimental show-jumping competition in Norfolk.

136

Above: Digger, the trainee Drum Horse, has a well-deserved but windy wander on Holkham Beach.
Opposite page: Open Weekend at Regimental Training is hugely popular with families and the general public. ***From top***: The Main Arena, the Musical Ride and the public visiting the stables.

Opposite: Captain Des Payne clears the last in the Regimental show jumping competition.

This page top: The 'Green' Exercise. Not for window cleaning! Ladders form an essential part of the break-in process in FIBUA (Fighting In Built Up Areas) training. *Middle*: Having blown a mousehole charge, soldiers assault a building. *Bottom*: Troopers undergo a hot debrief from the Directing Staff; the NCOs at the Mounted Regiment have a huge wealth of operational experience and are ideal mentors for the younger soldiers.

Tent Pegging. This is an ancient sport and comes as part of mounted skill-at-arms. Riders use lances to skewer and carry small wooden pegs (foreground) at the gallop. Originally the skill was used when raiding the enemy's tented camp as a shock tactic.

The Blues and Royals Squadron hacks out on Holkham Beach, one of the most unspoilt and beautiful stretches of sand in the country.

'Setting Sail.' Initially some of the horses are very wary of the waves but soon get used to it; two troopers head out into The Wash.

This page: Crowd Training in Norfolk. The horses and men go back to basics and get used to working with the carriages of the Royal Mews, Mounted Police and the noise of the bands.

Opposite: The Handy Hunter Competition. This cross country course provides a huge challenge for soldiers whose riding is mostly done on parade. Speedy decision-making and a tough resolve is a must for a successful round.

The Commanding Officer awards first prize to Major Nick van Cutsem and Squadron Corporal Major Byron Gibson after victory in the Handy Hunter.

147

CHAPTER 9

Standards of Excellence

The Mounted Regiment's size and structure is determined by the ceremonial requirements of providing the daily Queen's Life Guard and Escorts for State Occasions. The year at Knightsbridge follows a well-established pattern; December, January and February are dominated by training of both horses and soldiers, but in March the Squadrons start drills in preparation for the coming ceremonial season known to the troops as 'Silly Season'. Outside of this intense period however, the Regiment remains extremely busy with many other commitments.

The Combined Cavalry Memorial Parade takes place in the heart of Hyde Park in May. Representatives from all the cavalry regiments of the British Army, dressed in suits and bowler hats, and carrying tightly furled umbrellas, form up behind their regimental banners and march past the Cavalry Memorial. The salute is usually taken by a member of the Royal Family and, as the most senior cavalry regiments, The Life Guards and The Blues and Royals head the parade and provide a dismounted band and marching party.

During the Royal Windsor Horse Show in late May, Household Cavalrymen compete for the Richmond Cup which is presented annually by Her Majesty The Queen to the Mounted

Regiment's best turned out Trooper. The Household Cavalry is also involved in the Windsor Castle Royal Tattoo, which for the past three years has been staged during the Royal Windsor Horse Show. In 2012, we played a major role in a unique event in its place: the Diamond Jubilee Pageant, a celebration of The Queen's love of horses and her visits to foreign countries in the service of the United Kingdom.

Every November, the Mounted Regiment provides a dismounted division for the Remembrance Parade at the Cenotaph and, for the Lord Mayor's Parade, we field a mounted band and a mounted division, who spend six hours in the saddle, making it the most gruelling but most colourful parade of the year.

The Regiment enjoys a rewarding relationship with the local community. For this reason we are always pleased to host visits by a wide range of people from senior officers, politicians, neighbours and special interest groups – to our friends and family. From time to time, we are proud and honoured to be visited by members of the Royal Family.

The Princess Royal, Colonel of The Blues and Royals, visits the Warrant Officers' and NCOs' Mess at Hyde Park Barracks.

Previous page: Captain Simon Lukas 'cutting' on the Major General's Inspection. Words of command are replaced by the Divisional Commander signalling with his sword blade to direct his division.

Opposite: Her Majesty The Queen, accompanied by the Commanding Officer, awards the prizes for the Princess Elizabeth Cup (also known as the Richmond Cup) on the final day of the Royal Windsor Horse Show.

The Deputy Commander of London District, Brigadier Matthew Lowe, inspects Trooper Fisher and his horse, Goliath, during the Richmond Cup competition.

After weeks of cleaning kit to perfection, the Troopers are inspected in minute detail in the first round of the Richmond Cup.

The Garrison Sergeant Major, WO1 'Billy' Mott, gets into the detail while inspecting a Richmond Cup contestant.

Trooper Morrison wins the 2012 competition. Here, he is presented with the prize by The Queen: a hugely proud moment for him, his Troop and his Squadron.

This page top: On the first Sunday of May each year the officers and soldiers of the Household Cavalry and the Royal Armoured Corps meet in Hyde Park to march past the Cavalry Memorial and attend an open-air service of remembrance. Tradition dictates that Officers and Warrant Officers must parade in a sober suit, stiff-collared shirt and bowler hat, carrying a black, furled, cane-handled umbrella. *Bottom*: Wreaths are laid on Cavalry Memorial Sunday for those who lost their lives in the 1982 IRA bombing of the Queen's Life Guard on South Carriage Drive.

Opposite: The Blues and Royals (top) and The Life Guards (bottom) provide a guard of honour at the Cenotaph on Remembrance Sunday.

Above: A division of The Blues and Royals marches through the streets of the City of London escorting the Lord Mayor on his annual parade, The Lord Mayor's Show. First performed in 1215, the Show is for the newly elected Lord Mayor to pledge his allegiance to the Crown. Londoners from all walks of life come together to enjoy this splendid celebration of the City's tradition and future.

Opposite top: Her Royal Highness The Countess of Wessex meets Digger, a trainee Drum Horse who towers over all at a gargantuan 19.3 hands high. ***Below***: The Princess Royal, Gold Stick and Colonel of The Blues and Royals, is introduced to the newly trained Mercury by the Riding Master, Captain Mark Avison.

The Officers' Mess were delighted to have His Royal Highness the Duke of Cambridge back among their number with his new wife, Her Royal Highness the Duchess of Cambridge. The Mess presented Their Royal Highnesses with a commemorative painting as a wedding gift.

CHAPTER 10

Off Duty

Individual and team sports play an important part in our off duty hours. Naturally, these activities include show jumping and cross-country competitions as well as rugby, football, boxing and other sports only requiring two legs. Whilst we may be amateurs, we take our fun seriously, competing across the country at national levels as well as at internal military events. One of the most eagerly anticipated events in the sporting calendar is the annual Regimental football match which pits Officers & Troopers against the NCOs. We would hesitate to call it a grudge match but there are always plenty of thrills and spills!

Mess life is integral to the Regiment's ethos: dinner nights and other events are held regularly in both the Officers' Mess and the Warrant Officers' and NCOs' Mess. These nights can be both formal and informal affairs giving Mess members an opportunity to invite friends and family into their respective Messes, to enjoy a taste of Regimental tradition.

Then, of course, there are the pure off-duty moments of which the most long-established is the annual Brick Hanging ceremony which dates back to 1889 and takes place just before Christmas. The story (one of many, all of them plausible) is that Joe Holland, a civilian forage master to the 2nd Life Guards, was about to join the Senior NCOs for a pre-Christmas drink

Left: The annual Officers & Troopers vs NCOs football match reaches a head when the skills of Corporal of Horse Ruel Francis are pitted against the aggression of Trooper Wincott and the enthusiasm of Captain Alex Owen.

prior to going on leave. On the way, he was summoned to go instead to join the Commanding Officer for a sherry. None too pleased and seeing a loose brick in the corner of the Guardroom wall, he pulled it out and threw it up onto the sloping roof of the building, proclaiming to some NCOs present that, whilst it stayed up there he wanted the mess bar to remain open; 'I'll be back!' A few sherries later, and slightly the worse for wear, he went home to sleep off the effects. In due course he awoke, and suddenly remembered his request and dashed back into barracks to find the mess bar still open! Thereafter, a brick was 'hung' annually by Joe himself until his death in 1934. Each subsequent 'Brick Hanger' (usually the oldest living ex-Regimental Corporal Major who has not taken a commission) is issued with the 'Brick Hangers' medal.

Left: 'Give them great meals of beef and iron and steel, they will eat like wolves and fight like devils.' The Warrant Officers and NCOs settle in for the night after the State of the Nation Dinner.

'A kaleidoscope of tradition.'
The Officers host their fathers
in the Mess surrounded by 350
years of history in paintings,
silver and gold.

165

This page top: Major 'Tadge' Tate is crowned victorious at the end of a tough fight. **Bottom**: Brick Hanging. WO1 Esther Freeborn, the first female Bandmaster, takes down the brick after a long session in the Warrant Officers' and NCOs' Mess. The privilege of taking the brick down is reserved for the last person standing.

Opposite top left: 'A Fall from Gustavus.' Major Nana Twumasi-Ankhra takes a tumble from Gustavus at the 18th and final hedge during the Mounted Regiments' Cross Country Ride, held annually in Leicestershire. This immortal image created universal glee throughout the ranks of The Blues and Royals and on the pages of *Horse and Hound*. **Top right**: Captain Fred Hopkinson (left) awards the trophy to the race winner, Captain Billy Morley (right). **Bottom**: 'More leg!' Captain Alex Owen (rear) puts pressure on some of the civilian competitors, having only passed out of Riding School three months before.

'A Sea of Red and Gold.' The Warrant Officers and NCOs listen to the Commanding Officer as he addresses them at the annual State of the Nation Dinner.

Above: 'A run in the Park.' With either Hyde Park or Windsor Great Park on the Regiments' doorsteps, the soldiers train in some of the most picturesque postcodes in the UK. Here a troop runs up the Long Walk from Windsor Castle to the Copper Horse statue of George III. ***Opposite top***: The Officers' Mess uncharacteristically dressed down at Regimental Training in Norfolk. ***Bottom***: 'The Pain Train.' A Physical Training Instructor surveys his world with a smile as he orders 'just one more set', for the third time.

Christmas at Hyde Park Barracks. At Christmas, the Queen's Life Guard are inspected in fancy dress, with the best reliefs given to those who have made the most effort. In 2011, Trooper Palmer became No. 1 Boxman with his WWI Cavalryman's uniform. He has won competitions across the country for his rigid adherence to all things 1940s.

LSgt Sessing takes on Captain Fred Hopkinson during the annual Officers & Troopers vs NCOs football match.

Opposite top: Spartacus, after many years of service, is returned to his previous owner for retirement. *Bottom*: Rumour, at home with her adopted foal, was retired to be a foster mother.

This page top: 'Just William.' *Right*: Thomas, the Regiment's oldest horse at 24 years of age, is famous for his affection. The lads will miss his kisses when he retires in 2012.

CHAPTER 11

The Mounted Bands

Music is a very important part of military life. From the earliest days of warfare, armies have marched into battle to the skirl of the pipes, the music of the fifes and the beat of drums. From virtually the date of our formation to the present day, each of the Regiments of the Household Cavalry have had their own mounted bands: the only mounted bands of their kind and unrivalled in the world. Both are designated as State Bands and, when on parade with a member of the Royal Family present, wear 'gold coats' and velvet jockey caps whose design dates from the seventeenth century.

Each band is led by a Drum Horse, whose duty it is to carry the ornate silver kettledrums and State Trumpeters riding grey horses as ordered by King James II. To reach the peak of musical perfection, each band spends many hours in the rehearsal rooms. Rehearsals for the ceremonial season culminate with an inspection by the Commanding Officer of the Mounted Regiment.

In addition to State Ceremonial, the Mounted Bands parade on the Queen's Life Guard and, in 2012, they accompanied a detachment of the Royal Canadian Mounted Police on parade in London. When not on ceremonial duties, our bands, together with State Trumpeters and at least one of our Drum Horses, combine with twenty-four specially selected soldiers and horses to form the Musical Ride of the Household Cavalry.

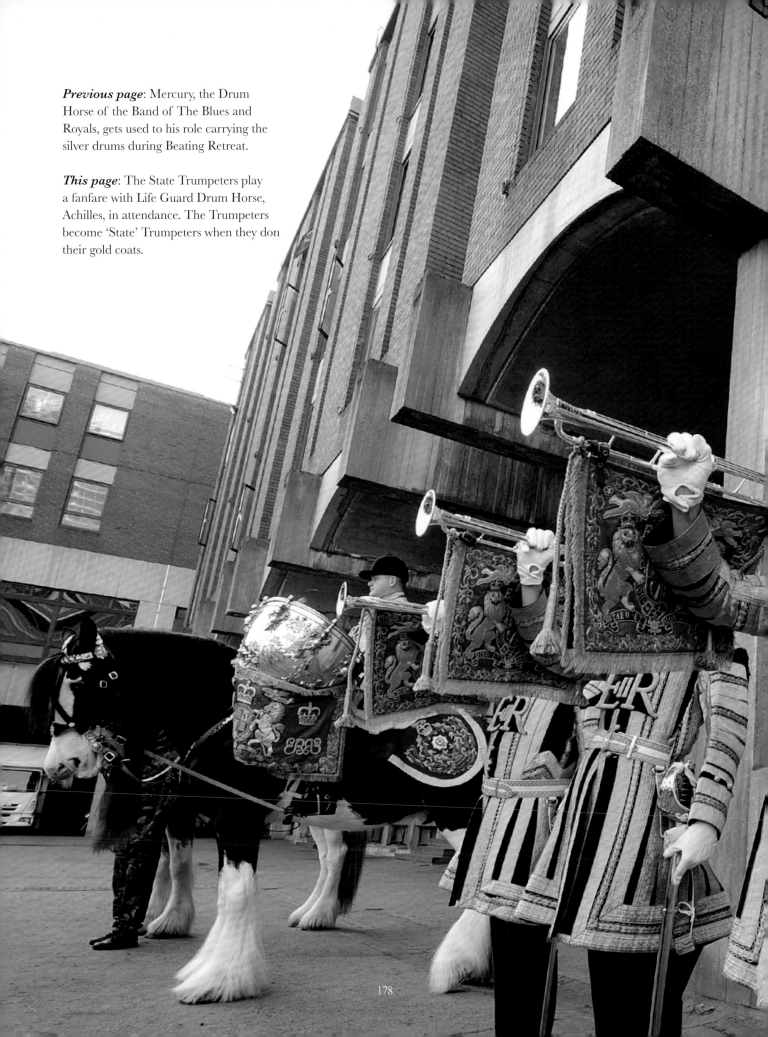

Previous page: Mercury, the Drum Horse of the Band of The Blues and Royals, gets used to his role carrying the silver drums during Beating Retreat.

This page: The State Trumpeters play a fanfare with Life Guard Drum Horse, Achilles, in attendance. The Trumpeters become 'State' Trumpeters when they don their gold coats.

178

Musical Rides or Quadrilles have been performed by horsed cavalry regiments since the 19th century. Today, we are the only Regular Army cavalry regiment to maintain that tradition and, consequently, are in high demand. Each year our Musical Ride performs at county shows and military tournaments across the country. In 2012, they are taking part in shows at Chatsworth, Holkham and Floors Castle. In 2009, the Musical Ride performed in Abu Dhabi and in 2013 we hope it will tour the United States.

Right: The Director of Music of the Band of The Life Guards leads the Double Mounted band of the Household Cavalry on the String Band rehearsal for The Queen's Birthday Parade. A Double Mounted band is comprised of 53 musicians and horses including two Drum Horses.
Below: Digger, the biggest horse in the UK, is exercised by a member of the Riding Staff.

The Piccolo; a female member
of the Band of The Life Guards
rehearses for The Queen's
Birthday Parade. Band members
need to adapt to riding and playing
at the same time. No mean feat!

Opposite top: The Bandmaster, WO1 Esther Freeborn, grooms her grey, Dallas. Because of the Household Cavalry's combat role, currently females can only serve in the Regiment as musicians, administrators, medics or veterinary specialists. *Below:* Achilles is prepared for a parade with his drummer, Lance Corporal D'Arcy, already in the saddle. Captain Alex Owen passes on his way to assume command of the Queen's Life Guard.

This page top: 'One hand on the reins, one hand on the tuba' – a member of the Band of The Blues and Royals. *Right*: The Band of The Life Guards play in their dismounted role at Hyde Park Barracks.

The Double Mounted Band of the
Household Cavalry move into position
while still playing during the Major
General's Inspection in Hyde Park.

The Musical Ride

The Musical Ride has been a part of the public face of the Household Cavalry for many years having first performed at The Royal Tournament in 1882. The routine is based on a series of cavalry drill movements set to music, and has changed very little over the years.

The soldiers on the Musical Ride wear exactly the same uniforms as those worn by the Household Cavalry Mounted Regiment on parade, but lances take the place of swords. Four members of the Ride wear stable dress that dates from the 1820s, and which is considerably less constricting than the full ceremonial uniform.

Unencumbered by heavy breast plates and plumed helmets, they are able to demonstrate traditional Household Cavalry skills. It takes four months of practice to get their horses to lie down (and stay down) at their command – a demonstration that recalls the days when horses went to battle and a rider trained his mount to lie down so that he could shelter behind it.

The Musical Ride forms in March to allow two months of hard training before public performances begin in May. The men are chosen for their ability to ride well, and the horses selected for their temperament and athleticism. It is not unusual for a very young trooper to join the Ride even though he may only have ridden for a matter of months.

Right: The world famous 'Musical Ride' at the Olympia Horse Show. Lance Corporal Glass, one of the Riding Staff's 'Monkey Men', performs in front of an audience of thousands.

Opposite top: A whirl of red and blue as the Musical Ride wheel around the Drum Horse in the centre of the show ring in Abu Dhabi. *Bottom*: Part of an intense routine of crossing, charging and reforming; nearly all of the display is in canter. The imposing black horses and armour-clad, lance-wielding soldiers canter within touching distance of the crowd to a stirring soundtrack with the sun glinting off bare steel.

This page top: Lance Corporal Heeley has the honour of galloping through the arena carrying the Union Flag as part of the finale, to 'Land of Hope and Glory'; it never fails to earn a standing ovation. *Below*: Lance Corporal Bishop lays down his horse George as the rest of the Ride circle around them. Only eight horses are trained as 'lie-down' horses.

Troopers Gasan and Hagley canter past Holkham Hall during a display at the Holkham Country Fair.

191

CHAPTER 12

For our Colonel-in-Chief

If you ask a British soldier in Afghanistan who he is fighting for, the answer is always, "my mates". Ask him who else, and next on the list, slightly further up the constitutional scale, is always, "The Queen". The Armed Forces enjoy a very special relationship with Her Majesty and this is especially true of the Household Cavalry. We have been protecting the Sovereign and fighting in Britain's conflicts continuously for over 350 years since Charles II and the Restoration of the Monarchy. At the last Diamond Jubilee, Queen Victoria's in 1897, we were performing the same task, in the same uniforms, riding similar horses. Queen Elizabeth II's Diamond Jubilee felt like a moment of destiny for the current Officers and soldiers of the Household Cavalry.

2012 was always going to be a busy year and the build-up was intense. April, one of the wettest on record, had threatened the cancellation of the Royal Windsor Horse Show. We battled through thick mud to perform at the Diamond Jubilee Pageant in Windsor where we had the privilege of escorting Her Majesty in to the arena in a stirring recreation of the 1953 Coronation Procession, a fitting tribute as well as a magnificent and unique experience for us all.

In May, Her Majesty saw fit to celebrate the Commonwealth by inviting the Royal Canadian Mounted Police to take part in British ceremonial events, re-enacting a gesture made by her father, King George VI, in 1936. The Mounties took the place of The Life Guards on duty at Whitehall for the Queen's Life Guard, performing a centuries-old tradition, for one day only, just the second non-British unit to have been awarded this honour.

We rehearsed hard for the Diamond Jubilee Carriage Procession and the horses were fit and well. On the day itself London was out in full patriotic force for the crowning moment of the Jubilee celebrations. The hours of work and preparation were reflected in glinting breastplates, gleaming leatherwork and jangling bright chains as we made our way to Westminster Hall. The jubilant crowds roared as we escorted Her Majesty in the 1902 State Landau, used by the Duke and Duchess of Cambridge on their wedding day last April, and over a million overjoyed onlookers cheered and waved at the great panoply of state on show. The sound was deafening, yet our soldiers and horses rose to the occasion, delivering Her Majesty to Buckingham Palace in the style which only a Sovereign's Escort can produce, and a spectacle which could only have happened in London. It truly was Uniquely British.

Back at Hyde Park Barracks, and as a final mark of respect and affection, we held our state helmets aloft and completed an historic day, and remarkable year, with a resounding three cheers for Her Majesty The Queen.

Previous page: The Diamond Jubilee Carriage Procession on the Mall. *Above*: Captain Thomas Davie leads the Captain's Escort at the Diamond Jubilee Pageant in the grounds of Windsor Castle. *Opposite*: Making history. The Mounties pass underneath Wellington Arch on the way to Horse Guards to take over the duties of the Queen's Life Guard for 24 hours.

This page top: Crowds throng in front of Buckingham Palace as the Red Arrows perform the closing act of an historic and remarkable weekend of celebration. ***Above left***: The Duke and Duchess of Cambridge travel in a State Landau from the Royal Mews. ***Above right***: The Mounted Regiment waiting to leave Hyde Park Barracks for the Diamond Jubilee Carriage Procession. ***Opposite***: 5am and four hours since reveille. The Early Morning Rehearsal finally gets under way.

The Blues and Royals lead the Carriage Procession.

Her Majesty The Queen, accompanied by the Prince of Wales and the Duchess of Cornwall, round the Queen Victoria Memorial.

Left: The Mounted Bands of the Household Cavalry announce the start of the procession on Whitehall.
Opposite: The Captain of the Queen's Life Guard orders the Royal Salute.

The Field Officer of the
Escort accompanies Her
Majesty along Whitehall.

"Three cheers for Her Majesty The Queen!". The Regiment shows its respect and admiration for Her Majesty on returning from the Diamond Jubilee Carriage Procession.

203

IN CONCLUSION

by Lieutenant Colonel Dan Hughes, Commanding Officer
Household Cavalry Mounted Regiment

It is our unique privilege at the Household Cavalry Mounted Regiment to carry out mounted and dismounted ceremonial duties on all State and Royal occasions, maintaining a world-famous tradition dating back to 1660, and forming an iconic part of our national heritage and military tradition. Yet the troops you see participating in ceremonial parades are fully-trained fighting troops, who may only recently have been operating armoured vehicles in the harsh terrain of Afghanistan. As this book concludes there are a few thoughts I would like to leave you with.

Firstly, that every Household Cavalryman is dual-trained in the ceremonial and armoured roles, a unique mix that calls for soldiers who can adapt to the added responsibility and variety that a career in the Household Cavalry offers. We rely on intelligent, fit and self-reliant soldiers who have the quick wits and initiative to succeed on operations, and achieve excellence in all they do, whether on horseback in London or in armoured vehicles in Iraq or Afghanistan. And when Afghanistan is just a memory, Household Cavalrymen are sure to be engaged in other combat zones.

Secondly, that whilst most people regard the ceremonial role as a glamorous one, the reality is a little different. The tempo of activity at the Mounted Regiment is intense, especially for the junior soldiers, most of whom have had little or no previous horse experience. Limited time off, long hours, early mornings and repetitive and frequent guard duties make for a tough routine. Our soldiers do an excellent job and we should never take for granted the hard work they put in to ensuring that such high standards are maintained.

Finally, and this is true of all Household Cavalrymen, we pursue excellence in everything we do, and see ourselves as guardians of the highest standards of military tradition. We cover a diverse set of tasks and do a vast amount of work to produce one of the most iconic elements of British military heritage. We also have a worldwide reputation for excellence. This reputation and the public support it engenders depends on us maintaining very high levels of professionalism, individual behaviour and self-discipline. We never take it for granted and strive to build on what our forebears have done, whether as fighting soldiers or as ceremonial troops. The versatility required to adapt to different roles – and the exacting standards to achieve success in both – has made the Household Cavalry what it is today and will help it face the challenges that lie ahead.